Quotations, Commas and Other Things English

Woodroof's Quotations, Commas and Other Things English

Instructor's Reference Edition

David K. Woodroof

iUniverse, Inc.
New York Lincoln Shanghai

Woodroof's
Quotations, Commas and Other Things English
Instructor's Reference Edition

Copyright © 2005 by David K. Woodroof

All rights reserved. No part of this book may be used or reproduced by any means, graphic, electronic, or mechanical, including photocopying, recording, taping or by any information storage retrieval system without the written permission of the publisher except in the case of brief quotations embodied in critical articles and reviews.

iUniverse books may be ordered through booksellers or by contacting:

iUniverse
2021 Pine Lake Road, Suite 100
Lincoln, NE 68512
www.iuniverse.com
1-800-Authors (1-800-288-4677)

ISBN-13: 978-0-595-36298-1 (pbk)
ISBN-13: 978-0-595-80738-3 (ebk)
ISBN-10: 0-595-36298-2 (pbk)
ISBN-10: 0-595-80738-0 (ebk)

Printed in the United States of America

Foreword

In the real world- -at home, at school, at the work place- - people need easy-to-understand answers to their grammar questions. *Quotations, Commas and Other Things English* provides a quick, accurate, and concise reference for presenting quotations, for the proper placement of commas, and for handling other often-mentioned problems with punctuation and composition.

The author is a former wire service reporter and award-winning newspaper editorial writer and editor. In 1995, he returned to the college classroom where he directs an English writing lab and continues to teach composition and literature.

Contents

QUOTATIONS

1. Quotation and Attribution Standing
   Alone as a Sentence 1
   - 1a. Quotation Followed by Attribution 2
   - 1b. Quotation Preceded by an Unquoted Word,
     Phrase(s), or Clause 2
   - 1c. Attribution Introduces Quotation 3
   - 1d. Attribution Introduces Formal or Long Quotation 3
   - 1e. Attribution within a Single Sentence 4
   - 1f. Attribution between Complete Sentences 5
   - 1g. Multiple Sentences before the Attribution 5
   - 1h. Introduced by a Complete Sentence 6

2. Quotation as Part of a Larger Sentence 7
   - 2a. Quote is a Complete Sentence 8
   - 2b. Quote as Predicate Nominative 8
   - 2c. Quote as Predicate Adjective 8
   - 2d. Quote as Object of Preposition 8
   - 2e. Quote as Direct Object 9
   - 2f. Quote as Indirect Object 9
   - 2g. Quote as Restrictive Appositive 9
   - 2h. Quote as Nonrestrictive Appositive 9

Woodroof's Quotations, Commas and Other Things English

    2i.   Quote Preceded by *That* Inserted into
a Larger Sentence 9

    2j.   Concluding Quoted Word or Phrase 10

3.   Quotation Marks with Periods, Commas, Colons,
Semicolons, Question Marks, Exclamation Points 10

    3a.   Periods Always Go inside Quotation Marks 10

    3b.   Commas Always Go inside Quotation Marks 12

    3c.   Colons Always Go outside Quotation Marks 12

    3d.   Semicolons Always Go outside Quotation Marks 12

    3e.   Question Mark with Quotation Marks 12

    3f.   Exclamation Point with Quotation Marks 13

    3g.   Question Mark or Exclamation Point 13

4.   Parentheses, Dashes,
or Commas with Quoted Material 14

    4a.   Quoted Sentence Inserted Using Parentheses 14

    4b.   Quoted Fragment inside Parentheses 15

    4c.   Freestanding Parentheses 16

    4d.   Quoted Sentence Inserted Using Dashes 16

    4e.   Quoted Fragment inside Dashes 17

    4f.   Quoted Sentence Inserted Using Commas 18

    4g.   Quoted Fragment inside Commas 19

5.   Brackets 20

    5a.   Brackets in Quotations 20

    5b.   Brackets with *Sic* 20

    5c.   Brackets inside Parentheses 21

6.   Ellipsis 21

    6a.   Ellipsis Dots at the Beginning or End of a Quotation 21

    6b.   Omission Using *That* in Place of Ellipsis Dots 23

    6c.   Word(s) Omitted from the Middle of a Sentence 23

    6d.   Word(s) Omitted from the End of a Sentence 24

6e.	Sentence Ending with an Omission and a Source Citation	25
6f.	Omission of Sentence(s)	26
6g.	Omission of Paragraphs(s)	27
6h.	Ellipsis Dots and Poetry	28
6i.	Ellipsis Dots after an Unfinished Sentence	29

7. Long Quotation Formats: Block or Rolling 30
   - 7a. Block Format 30
   - 7b. Rolling Format 32

8. Dialogue 33
   - 8a. Exterior Dialogue 33
   - 8b. Dashes with Dialogue 35
   - 8c. Ellipsis as an Alternative for the Dash 36
   - 8d. Interior Dialogue 36

9. When Quotations Are Not Preceded by a Comma 37
   - 9a. After a Linking Verb 38
   - 9b. After Gerund Object of Preposition 38
   - 9c. After an Infinitive 39
   - 9d. Exception to the Exceptions 39

10. Adages, Axioms, Maxims, Mottoes, Proverbs, Rules, Sayings, Truisms 40
    - 10a. Hints for Handling Adages That Are Appositives 41

11. Freestanding Epigrams, Epigraphs and Quotations 41

12. Indirect Quotation 42

COMMAS

13. Commas with Absolute Phrases 45

14. *A, An, The* as Adjectives in a Series 46

15. No Comma Before the First Adjective in a Series 46

16. No Comma after the Final Adjective in a Series 46

17. Numbers as Adjectives in a Series 46

18. Commas with Addresses 47

19. Commas with Direct Address 47

20. Commas with Adverbial Clauses 47

21. Commas with *As, Since* 48

22. Commas for Clarity 48

23. Commas When Compound Subject has Positive and Negative Elements 49

24. Commas, Conjunctions, and Compound Items in a Series 49

25. Comma Use before a Concluding Dependent Clause 50

26. Commas with Contrasting Elements 50

27. Commas with Coordinating Conjunctions *(Fan Boys)* 51

28. Commas with Dates 51

29. Commas with Degrees and Titles 52

30. Commas with Infinitive Phrases 53

31. Commas with Participial Phrases 53

32. Commas with Prepositional Phrases 54

33. Commas with Place Names 54

34. Series Using Only Commas 54

35. Series Using Only Conjunctions 55

36. Series of Names in a Firm's Title 55

37. Never Place Commas after *Such As* or *Like* 55

38. Commas with Social Salutation and Close 56

39. Commas with a Tag Question 56

40. Comma When *That* Is Understood 56

41. Commas to Set Off Transposed Modifiers 57

42. Comma in Place of Word(s) Omitted 57

43. Commas with Words, Phrases, or Clauses in a Series 58

44. Commas with *Yes, No,* and Other Responses 58

45. Direct Question 59

46. Question Mark in Brackets or Parentheses to Express Doubt 60

47. Abbreviation *c.* Before a Date That Is in Doubt 61

48. Indirect Question 61

49. Correcting Comma Splices and Run-on Sentences 62
    49a. Correct by Creating Two Separate Sentences 63
    49b. Correct with a Semicolon 63
    49c. Correct with a Colon 63
    49d. Correct by Subordinating an Independent Clause 63
    49e. Correct with a Semicolon, Conjunctive Adverb, and Comma 64
    49f. Correct with a Comma and Coordinating Conjunction 64

50. Rarely Used Comma Options 64

51. Pairings Testing to Punctuate Adjectives in a Series .. 65
    51a. Series Adjectives All Coordinate 66
    51b. Series Adjectives All Noncoordinate 67
    51c. Series Is a Mix of Coordinate and
         Noncoordinate Adjectives 67

52. Series Adjectives Modifying a Pronoun 68

53. Restrictive and Nonrestrictive Appositives,
    Clauses, Phrases 69
    53a. Restrictive Sentence Elements 70
    53b. Appositives and the Articles *A, An, The* 70
    53c. Nonrestrictive Sentence Elements 71
    53d. After Proper Nouns 71
    53e. After Preceding Modifiers 72
    53f. Preceding Appositive Phrase 73

54. *We* or *Us* Before a One-Word Appositive 73

55. Relative Pronouns *That* and *Which* 74

OTHER THINGS ENGLISH

56. *A, An*, before Consonant and
    Vowel Sounding Words 77

57. A.M., P.M. 77

58. Apostrophe 78
    58a. With Contractions 78
    58b. With Plurals 78

59. Capitalization 79
    59a. Common Nouns 79
    59b. Stand-Alone Personal Title 79

59c.	With Family Relationships	80
59d.	With Religion	80
59e.	With Geographical Areas and Directions	81
59f.	Days, Months, Holidays, Seasons	81
59g.	Titles	81
59h.	*AD* and *BC* or *CE* and *BCE*	82
59i.	Hyphenated Words in Titles	83

60. Collective Nouns and Verbs 83
    60a. *Number*: Singluar or Plural? 84
    60b. Fractional Number 84

61. Colon or Dash Introduces an Appositive, Explanation, or Series 85

62. Colon with a Verb or Preposition That Introduces a Series 85

63. Dash with Preceding Word or Series 86

64. Forming Plurals 86
    64a. Compound Word That Includes a Noun 87
    64b. Compound Word with Nouns of Equal Value 87
    64c. Compound Word with No Noun 88

65. Forming Possessives 88
    65a. Plural Noun 88
    65b. Individual Possession or Ownership 88
    65c. Joint Possession or Ownership 89
    65d. Animate Objects 89
    65e. Inanimate Objects 90
    65f. Compound Word 90
    65g. Indefinite Pronoun 91
    65h. Personal Pronoun 91
    65i. Pronouns Ending in *Self* or *Selves* 91

Woodroof's Quotations, Commas and Other Things English

66. Hyphen 91
    66a. Hyphens to Form Compound Adjectives 91
    66b. Hyphens Omitted between *-ly*, *-er*,
         or *-est* Ending Modifiers 92
    66c. Compound Adjectives with the Same Base Word 92
    66d. Compound Numbers, Fractions 93
    66e. Hyphenated Measurements 93
    66f. Measurement as Part of a Noun 94
    66g. Numbers with Ages 95
    66h. *Age* and *Aged* 95
    66i. Same Spelling But Different Words 95

67. Latin Abbreviations 96
    67a. *I.E.* (that is) 96
    67b. *E.G.* (for example) 97
    67c. *Etc.* (and so forth, and others) 98

68. Linking Verbs 98
    68a. Predicate Noun 99
    68b. Predicate Adjective 99
    68c. Predicate Pronoun 100

69. Literary Present Tense 101

70. Parentheses, Dashes,
    or Commas with Regular Material 101
    70a. Regular Sentence Inserted Using Parentheses 102
    70b. Regular Fragment inside Parentheses 103
    70c. Freestanding Parentheses 103
    70d. Regular Sentence Inserted Using Dashes 104
    70e. Regular Fragment inside Dashes 105
    70f. Regular Sentence Inserted Using Commas 105
    70g. Regular Fragment inside Commas 106

71.	Indefinite Pronouns	107
	71a. Exception I (Indefinite Pronouns That Are Always Plural)	108
	71b. Exception II (Indefinite Pronouns That Can Be Singular or Plural)	108
	71c. *None*: The Unique Indefinite Pronoun	109
	71d. Compound Subjects with *Each* or *Every*	109
	71e. Compound Subjects with *And*	110
	71f. Compound Subjects With *Or* or *Nor*	110
	71g. Pronoun Agreement with *Or* or *Nor*	111
	71h. *One of, Only one of, The only one of*	111
	71i. *One, One's; He, His; She, Her*	112
	71j. *Each Other, One Another*	112
	71k. Pronouns after *As* or *Than*	113
	71l. Intensive and Reflexive Pronouns	113
	71m. Pronoun Order in a Compound	114
	71n. Relative Pronouns *That* and *Which*	114
	71o. Determining the Correct Pronoun to join with a Noun or another Pronoun	114
	71p. Pronoun before a Gerund or Participle	115
72.	Slash	116
73.	Spacing with Punctuation	116
74.	Verb Tenses	117
	74a. Present Tense	118
	74b. Past Tense	118
	74c. Future Tense	119
	74d. Perfect Tenses	119
	74e. Present Perfect Tense	119
	74f. Past Perfect Tense	120
	74g. Future Perfect Tense	120

	74h.	Progressive Tenses 121
	74i.	Emphatic Tenses 121
75.	Underlining (Italics) Versus Quotation Marks for Names and Titles 122	
	75a.	Titles Underlined (Italicized) 122
	75b.	When *The* is the First Part of a Newspaper or Periodical Title Used in Text 123
	75c.	When a Geographic Name Begins a Newspaper or Periodical Title 123
	75d.	Names Underlined (Italicized) 123
	75e.	Nicknames 124
	75f.	Word, Phrase, Number, or Letter Discussed as Itself 124
	75g.	Word(s) Being Defined 125
	75h.	Foreign Words and Expressions 125
	75i.	Underlining (Italics) for Emphasis 125
	75j.	Your Own Title 125
	75k.	Titles within Quotation Marks 126
	75l.	Quotation Marks with Words Used in a Unique, Ironic, or Special Way. 126
	75m.	Do Not Use Quotation Marks with Cliches or Common Slang 126
	75n.	What Not to Underline (Italicize) or Place within Quotation Marks 127
76.	*Who, Whom,* and *Whose* 127	
	76a.	Parenthetic Expressions and the Choice of *Who* or *Whom* 127
	76b.	*Who/Whom*, Preposition, Infinitive, Dependent Clause 130
	76c.	*Who/Whom* and Regular Infinitives 131
	76d.	*Who/Whom* and the Infinitive *To Be* 132

QUOTATIONS

A quotation is the exact reproduction of words originally spoken or written by someone else. Quotation marks are the grammatical symbols that set quotations apart from other text. They are always used in pairs, double (" ") or single (' ') as appropriate.

Rules for the correct presentation of quoted material are essentially the same for all types of writing. Format requirements for academic papers do, however, dictate occasional variations in the treatment of quotations, and the most important of these will be discussed. While there are many academic formats, the styles established by the Modern Language Association (MLA) and the American Psychological Association (APA) are the most widely used. With few exceptions, MLA and the APA guidelines for quotations parallel the standards of traditional usage.

1. *Quotation and Attribution Standing Alone as a Sentence*

A whole sentence quotation can be seen as having two distinct parts: the quotation itself (the words spoken or written) and its attribution (who spoke it or wrote it). There are several basic structures for presenting whole-sentence quotations.

1a. *Quotation Followed by Attribution*

Arranged this way, the sentence begins with quotation marks and a capital letter. The quoted words end with the appropriate punctuation (comma, question mark, exclamation point, etc.) and quotation marks. The attribution ends with a period and is all lowercase unless it contains a proper noun, like Bob (example 4).

Examples

1. "There is a car," she said.
2. "Is that a car?" she asked.
3. "That is a car!" he yelled.
4. "That is a car!" Bob yelled.

1b. *Quotation Preceded by an Unquoted Word, Phrase(s), or Clause*

If a directly stated quotation is preceded by an unquoted word (example1), phrase (example 2), phrases (example 3), or dependent clause (example 4), the quotation begins with quote marks and a lower case letter whether the attribution is at the end or in the middle of the sentence as in examples 4 & 5.

Examples

1. Suddenly, "she bought her first boat," Bob said.
2. Using lottery money, "she bought her first boat," Bob said.
3. On a Monday in May, "she bought her first boat," Bob said.

4. After Mary won the lottery, "she bought her first boat," Bob said.
5. After Mary won the lottery, Bob said, "she bought her first boat."

1c. Attribution Introduces Quotation

When placed first, the attribution begins with a capital letter and ends with a comma. The quoted words begin with quotation marks and a capital letter and end with the appropriate punctuation and quotation marks.

<u>Examples</u>

1. She said, "There is a car."
2. She asked, "Is that a car?"
3. He yelled, "That is a car!"
4. Bob yelled, "That is a car!"

1d. Attribution Introduces Formal or Long Quotation

Use a colon rather than a comma after an attribution that introduces a formal or very long quotation (more than 40 words).

<u>Examples</u>

1. She said: "Our club charter is very clear that - ."
2. She asked: "Is that a car in - - - - - - - - - - - ?"
3. He exclaimed: "That is a car in - - - - - - - - !"
4. Bob exclaimed: "That is a car in - - - - - - - !"

1e. *Attribution within a Single Sentence*

The first segment of the sentence begins with quotation marks and a capital letter and ends with a comma and quotation marks. The attribution is all lowercase unless it contains a proper noun, like *Bob* (example 4), and it ends with a comma. The final segment begins with quotation marks and is all lowercase unless it contains a proper noun, like *Sue's* (example 3). It concludes with the appropriate punctuation and quotation marks. With a compound sentence whose independent clauses are joined by a semicolon, the attribution may come at the end (example 5) or in the middle (example 6). When the attribution is placed in the middle of a sentence (example 6), the first clause ends with a comma and quotation marks. A semicolon follows the attribution, and the second clause begins with quotation marks and a lowercase letter unless the first word is a proper noun.

Examples

1. "There is," she continued, "a car sitting in the middle of the yard."
2. "Is that," she asked, "a car sitting in the middle of the yard?"
3. "That is," he yelled, "Sue's car sitting in the middle of the yard!"
4. "That is," Bob yelled, "a car sitting in the middle of the yard!"
5. "There is a car; it is sitting in the middle of the yard," he said.
6. "There is a car," he said; "it is sitting in the middle of the yard."

1f. *Attribution between Complete Sentences*

The first sentence always begins with quotation marks and a capital letter. Its quoted words end with appropriate punctuation and closing quotation marks (examples 1-4).

The attribution ends with a period and is all lowercase unless it contains a proper noun, like *Bob* in example 4.

The first sentence following the attribution begins with quotation marks and a capital letter. Each additional sentence begins with a capital letter, but quotation marks are only placed after the end punctuation of the final sentence (examples 2, 3, 4).

Examples

1. "There is a police car," she said. "It is sitting in the middle of the yard."
2. "Is that a police car?" she asked. "We should call 911. Maybe it is stolen!"
3. "It is a police car!" he yelled. "I'm calling 911. I don't think I'm being unreasonable."
4. "It is a police car!" Bob yelled. "I'm calling 911. I don't think I'm being unreasonable."

1g. *Multiple Sentences before the Attribution*

As a writing alternative, up to three closely related sentences may be positioned in front of their attribution (example 1).

With this format, the first sentence begins with quotation marks and a capital letter. Each additional sentence begins with a capital letter, but closing quotation marks are only placed after the appropriate end punctuation (usually a comma) of the final sentence.

If there are quoted sentences following the attribution, the first one begins with quotation marks and a capital letter. Each additional sentence begins with a capital letter, but quotation marks are only placed after the end punctuation of the final sentence (example 2).

Examples

1. "I couldn't tell what it was at first. It was very dark outside. I realized later that it was a police car," she said.
2. "I couldn't tell what it was at first. It was very dark outside. I realized later that it was a police car," she said. "That's when we decided to call 911. The response was almost immediate. The police got here in less than five minutes."

1h. Introduced by a Complete Sentence

The introducing sentence, which always concludes with a colon, should identify the author of the quotation to be presented and the source from which it is taken (unless previously provided). The quoted material begins with quotation marks and a capital letter and concludes with appropriate punctuation and quotation marks.

Example

Naturalist John Doe, writing in <u>Feral Cats</u>, is intrigued by the dual nature of domestic felines: "Cats can be so independent and yet so loving at the same time."

NOTE: A sentence may conclude with a colon and introduce a regular sentence (one not in quotations) when the second sentence explains, expands on, or closely refers back to the first (example 1). The use of a capital letter to begin the second regular sentence is optional (example 2.) Whichever the choice, its use should be consistent throughout the same work.

Examples

1. Auto racing helmets are designed to prevent or reduce impact damage to the head: Helmets also protect against burn injuries to the face, head and neck.
2. Auto racing helmets are designed to prevent or reduce impact damage to the head: helmets also protect against burn injuries to the face, head and neck.

2. *Quotation as Part of a Larger Sentence*

When a quotation- -word, phrase, or complete sentence- -is only part of and not the substance of a larger sentence, it is punctuated according to the grammatical function it has in the larger sentence.

If the quotation is a complete sentence, it begins with a capital letter. Otherwise, the quotation is all lowercase except for proper nouns.

A quotation may function in a larger sentence as its subject or predicate nominative, a predicate adjective, object of preposition, direct object, indirect object, or as an appositive.

2a. *Quote is a Complete Sentence*

If a quoted sentence that originally ended with a period is inserted into the beginning or middle of another sentence, the opening and closing quotation marks are retained, but the period is deleted (example 1). If it originally ended with a question mark (example 2) or an exclamation point (example 3), that punctuation is retained within the closing quotation marks.

Examples

1. "Only the good die young" was George's favorite saying.
2. "Do only the good die young?" is a question asked by each generation.
3. "Only the good die young!" was the last thing we heard before George jumped.

2b. *Quote as Predicate Nominative*

Example

George's favorite saying was "Only the good die young."

2c. *Quote as Predicate Adjective*

Example

George was "green with envy."

2d. *Quote as Object of Preposition*

Example

The baseball was hit all the way to the children's "press box."

2e. *Quote as Direct Object*

Example

George gave "the good stuff" to his friend.

2f. *Quote as Indirect Object*

Example

George gave "the one-armed bandit" more than $6,000.

2g. *Quote as Restrictive Appositive*

Example

The old adage "Only the good die young" was better than any song to him.

2h. *Quote as Nonrestrictive Appositive*

Example

An old adage, "Only the good die young," was better than any song to him.

2i. *Quote Preceded by* **That** *Inserted into a Larger Sentence*

If the quotation is a word, phrase, or complete sentence and it is immediately preceded by the word *that*, it begins with a lowercase letter (example 1) unless its own first word is a proper noun (example 2). In either case, there is no comma before or after *that*.

Examples

1. He liked the old adage that "only the good die young."
2. He liked the old line that "Jack Sprat could eat no fat and his wife could eat no lean."

2j. Concluding Quoted Word or Phrase

Capitalize but do not set off by comma a concluding quoted word (example 1) or phrase (example 2) that follows an attribution and conveys the meaning of a complete sentence. (Otherwise, unless it begins a sentence, contains a proper noun, or was capitalized originally, a quoted word or phrase is all lowercase.)

For added emphasis, however, a concluding quoted word or phrase may be set off by comma (examples 3, 4).

Examples

1. Molly rolled her eyes and said "Possibly."
2. After a long pause, George answered "Not a chance."
3. Molly rolled her eyes and said, "Possibly."
4. After a long pause, George answered, "Not a chance."

3. Quotation Marks with Periods, Commas, Colons, Semicolons, Question Marks, Exclamation Points

3a. Periods Always Go inside Quotation Marks

The punctuation of quotations within quotations may be the best illustration of an important grammatical principle: Periods always go inside quotation marks. Recall that titles of entities considered parts of other works (e.g., short stories, articles, chapters, etc.) are enclosed with quotation marks. Titles of whole entities (e.g., novels, newspapers, books, etc.) are underlined.

There is an orderly process for punctuating quotations. Working outside inward, use double quotation marks (" ") to set off a stated quote (example 1) or quoted material (example 2). When a quotation has separate quoted material within itself (quote within a quote), set the second quotation off with a pair of single quote marks (' ') as shown in example 3.

If there is a third quote (quote within a quote within a quote), set it off with double quotation marks (example 4). A fourth quote (quote within a quote within a quote within a quote) would be set off with single quotation marks (examples 5,6), etc.

No matter how simple the quotation is (examples 1,2) or how complicated (examples 3-6), when a period is appropriate, it is always positioned inside the quotation marks whether they are double, single, or a combination of both.

<u>Examples</u>

Stated Quote

1. John said, "I just read a short story."

Quoted Material

2. John just read the short story "Jelly Bean Ride."

Quote within a Quote

3. John said, "I just read the short story 'Jelly Bean Ride.' "

Quote within a Quote within a Quote

4. John said, "Joe stated, 'I just read the short story "Jelly Bean Ride."' "

Quote within a Quote within a Quote within a Quote

5. John said, "Joe stated, 'Yesterday Sue reported, "I too have just read the short story 'Jelly Bean Ride.' " ' "
6. John said, "Joe stated, 'Yesterday Sue reported, "I too have just read the short story 'Jelly Bean Ride' and really enjoyed it." ' "

3b. *Commas Always Go inside Quotation Marks*

Example

I just read the short story "Jelly Bean Ride," and I enjoyed it.

3c. *Colons Always Go outside Quotation Marks*

Example

I just read the short story "Jelly Bean Ride": it is now my favorite John Doe work.

3d. *Semicolons Always Go outside Quotation Marks*

Example

I just read the short story "Jelly Bean Ride"; fortunately, it is not difficult to understand.

3e. *Question Mark with Quotation Marks*

If the quoted words themselves ask a question, the question mark is placed inside the closing quotation marks (example 1). Otherwise, place the question mark outside the closing quotation marks (example 2).

Examples

1. Did John say, "Am I here?" ("Am I here?" is a question)
2. Did John say, "I am here"? ("I am here" is a statement.)

3f. *Exclamation Point with Quotation Marks*

If the quoted words themselves are exclamatory, place the exclamation point inside the closing quotation marks (example 1). Otherwise, place the exclamation point outside the closing quotation marks (example 2).

Examples

1. While pounding his fists on the table, John shouted, "There is no one else in the world as smart as I am!" (Structured this way, the quotation is exclamatory.)
2. A pox on the silly person who believes, "There is no one else in the world as smart as I am"! (Structured this way, the quotation is merely a statement, but the sentence as a whole is exclamatory.

3g. *Question Mark or Exclamation Point*

When the nature of a sentence or quotation is both interrogative and exclamatory, the choice of a question mark or an exclamation point as its punctuation is a matter of emphasis.

Examples

1. "Aren't you ever going to pay your debts?" he asked.
2. "Aren't you ever going to pay your debts!" he screamed.

4. *Parentheses, Dashes, or Commas with Quoted Material*

Quoted material can be set off from regular text using parentheses, dashes, or commas. Parentheses provide the least emphasis, dashes the most emphasis, and commas are used to present material whose importance lies somewhere in between.

4a. *Quoted Sentence Inserted Using Parentheses*

Parentheses, upright curved lines ( ), are always used in pairs, one before and one after the material they enclose. A comma is never placed before an opening parenthesis, but it may be used after a closing parenthesis.

The inserted sentence is preceded by an opening parenthesis and begins with quotation marks and a capital letter. It concludes with quotation marks and a closing parenthesis. If a quoted sentence that originally ended with a period is inserted somewhere in the middle of another sentence, the opening and closing quotation marks are retained, but the period is deleted (example 1). If it originally ended with a question mark (example 2) or an exclamation point (example 3), that punctuation is retained and followed by quotation marks and a closing parenthesis. If the insertion concludes a sentence, the appropriate end punctuation (e.g., period, question mark, or exclamation point) is placed after the concluding parenthesis (example 4).

Examples

1. The bride's father was so happy ("The bride and groom are a picture-perfect couple") that he even danced with his new in-laws.
2. The bride's father was so happy ("Aren't the bride and groom a picture-perfect couple?") that he even danced with his new in-laws.
3. The bride's father was so happy ("My daughter and new son-in-law look like movie stars!") that he even danced with his new in-laws.
4. The bride's father was so happy ("My daughter and new son-in-law look like movie stars!").

4b. *Quoted Fragment inside Parentheses*

A quoted fragment is treated like a quoted sentence when it is inserted into another sentence using parentheses except that a fragment is all lowercase unless it contains proper nouns. If the quoted fragment was originally followed by a period, it is placed within quotation marks, but the period is deleted (example 1). If it originally ended with a question mark (example 2) or an exclamation point (example 3), that punctuation is retained and followed by quotation marks and a closing parenthesis. If the insertion concludes a sentence, the appropriate end punctuation is placed after its closing parenthesis (example 4).

Examples

1. The bride's father ("an odd individual_") pretended that he was happy.
2. The bride's father ("a cousin of yours?") pretended that he was happy.
3. The bride's father ("a crafty old fox!") pretended that he was happy.
4. The bride's father reminded me of a sly forest creature ("a crafty old fox!")_.

4c. *Freestanding Parentheses*

A quoted sentence within freestanding parentheses begins with quotation marks and a capital letter. It retains its original end punctuation- -period, question mark, or exclamation point- -and concludes with quotation marks. No punctuation is placed outside freestanding parentheses.

Example

1. The bride's father was very happy. ("The bride and groom are a picture-perfect couple_.")

4d. *Quoted Sentence Inserted Using Dashes*

The dash is typed as two hyphens (- -) with no space between it and the text that precedes or follows it.

The inserted sentence is preceded by a dash and begins with quotation marks and a capital letter. It concludes with quotation marks and a dash.

If a quoted sentence that originally ended with a period is inserted somewhere in the middle of another sentence, the opening and closing quotation marks are retained, but the period is deleted (example 1). If it originally ended with a question mark (example 2) or an exclamation point (example 3), that punctuation is retained and followed by quotation marks and a dash. If it concludes a sentence (example 4), the insertion's closing dash is replaced by the appropriate end punctuation (e.g., period, question mark, or exclamation point) and followed by closing quotation marks.

Examples

1. The bride's father was so happy- -"The bride and groom are a picture-perfect couple"- -that he even danced with his in-laws.
2. The bride's father was so happy- -"Aren't the bride and groom a picture-perfect couple?"- -that he even danced with his in-laws.
3. The bride's father was so happy- -"My daughter and new son-in-law look like movie stars!"- -that he even danced with his new in-laws.
4. The bride's father was so happy- -"My daughter and new son-in-law look like movie stars!"

4e. Quoted Fragment inside Dashes

A quoted fragment is treated like a quoted sentence when it is inserted into another sentence using dashes except that a fragment is all lowercase unless it contains proper nouns. If the quoted fragment was originally followed by a period, it is placed within quotation marks, but the period is deleted (example 1). If it originally ended with a question mark (example 2) or an exclamation point (example 3), that punctuation is retained and followed by quotation marks and a dash. If it concludes a sentence (example 4), the insertion's closing dash is replaced by the appropriate end punctuation and followed by quotation marks.

Examples

1. The bride's father- -"an odd individual_"- -pretended he was happy.
2. The bride's father- -"a cousin of yours?"- -pretended that he was happy.
3. The bride's father- -"a crafty old fox!"- -pretended that he was happy.
4. The bride's father reminded me of a sly forest creature- -"a crafty old fox!"

4f. Quoted Sentence Inserted Using Commas

The inserted sentence is preceded by a comma and begins with quotation marks and a capital letter. If a quoted sentence that originally ended with a period is inserted into the middle of another sentence, the opening and closing quotation marks are retained, but the period is deleted and replaced by a comma (example 1).

If the inserted sentence originally ended with a question mark (example 2) or an exclamation point (example 3), that punctuation is retained and followed by quotation marks.

Examples

1. The bride's father was so happy, "The bride and groom are a picture-perfect couple," that he even danced with his in-laws.

2. The bride's father was so happy, "Aren't the bride and groom a picture-perfect couple?" that he even danced with his in-laws.
3. The bride's father was so happy, "My daughter and new son-in-law look like movie stars!" that he even danced with his new in-laws.

4g. *Quoted Fragment inside Commas*

A quoted fragment is treated like a quoted sentence when it is inserted into another sentence using commas except that a fragment is all lowercase unless it contains proper nouns. If a quoted fragment was originally followed by a period, it is placed within quotation marks, but the period is replaced by a comma (example 1). If it originally ended with a question mark (example 2) or an exclamation point (example 3), that punctuation is retained and followed by quotation marks. If it concludes a sentence (example 4), the insertion is followed by the appropriate end punctuation and closing quotation marks.

<u>Examples</u>

1. The bride's father, "an odd individual," pretended that he was happy.
2. The bride's father, "a cousin of yours?" pretended that he was happy.
3. The bride's father, "a crafty old fox!" pretended that he was happy.
4. The bride's father reminded me of a sly forest creature, "a crafty old fox!"

5. Brackets

5a. Brackets in Quotations

Use brackets [ ] to enclose explanatory, amplifying or correcting information when it is inserted into a quotation.

Examples

Explanatory Material
"That was the year [1492 when he finally received sufficient funding from Spain] that Columbus discovered the New World."

Amplifying Material
"That was the year [the prevailing winds in 1492 were the most favorable in a decade] that Columbus discovered the New World."

Correcting Material
"It was 1592 [actually, it was 1492] that Columbus discovered the New World," John said.

5b. Brackets with Sic

Sic is Latin for *thus* or *so*. In grammar, the word *sic* is enclosed in brackets and inserted into a quotation to note an error or mistake by the original speaker or writer.

Example

"It was 1592 [sic] that Columbus discovered the New World," John declared.

5c. *Brackets inside Parentheses*

Place brackets around parenthetic information when it is inserted into material already enclosed in parentheses.

Example

The summer of 1852 (according to the foremost expert [Dr. John Doe] on wind patterns) was the last time a sailing ship could go that far north without getting trapped in ice.

6. *Ellipsis*

The ellipsis mark, three spaced dots or periods (...), is used with quotations to indicate the omission of material from within a sentence, between sentences, or between paragraphs.

The use of ellipsis dots is an appropriate option when material can be deleted without changing the essential meaning or context of the original quotation.

Ellipsis dots are not used when a single quoted word, phrase, or fragment is integrated into another sentence (e.g., the drink was "on the house" and didn't cost me anything).

6a. *Ellipsis Dots at the Beginning or End of a Quotation*

Ellipsis dots are not normally used to mark a deletion from the beginning of the first (or only) sentence in a quotation (example 1) or to mark a deletion from the end of the final (or only) sentence in a quotation (example 2). Such abbreviated sentences are usually presented as regular full sentences.

However, ellipsis dots may be used in either case when for reasons of accuracy or clarity the author considers it is necessary to emphasize that a quotation begins in the middle of its first (or only) sentence or ends in the middle of its last (or only) sentence.

To mark a deletion at the beginning of the first (or only) sentence in a quotation, begin the abbreviated sentence with quotation marks, three ellipsis dots, and a capital letter (in brackets unless the first word is a proper noun). See example 3.

To mark a deletion at the end of the final (or only) sentence in a quotation, conclude the abbreviated sentence with the proper end punctuation (period, question mark, or exclamation point), three ellipsis dots, and closing quotation marks. See example 4. (Note also "Words Omitted from the End of a Sentence," page 24.)

<u>Examples</u>

Original Quotation: John Doe said, "Either with cash or by check, the tax bill I owe will definitely be paid before the November 15 deadline, which is still two weeks away."

Example 1: John Doe said, "The tax bill I owe will definitely be paid before the November 15 deadline, which is still two weeks away."

Example 2: John Doe said, "Either with cash or by check, the tax bill I owe will definitely be paid before the November 15 deadline."

Example 3: John Doe said, "...[T]he tax bill I owe will definitely be paid before the November 15 deadline, which is still two weeks away."

Example 4: John Doe said, "Either with cash or by check, the tax bill I owe will definitely be paid before the November 15 deadline...."

6b. *Omission Using* **That** *in Place of Ellipsis Dots*

When the word *that* introduces a new, shortened quoted sentence, it is not preceded by a comma or ellipsis dots <u>nor</u> is it followed by a comma. The first word in a quotation introduced by *that* should be lowercase (see abbreviated quotation) unless it is a proper noun.

<u>Example</u>

Original Quotation: John Doe said, "I know an amazingly high percentage of World War I deaths were related to the use of gas."

Abbreviated Quotation: John Doe said that "an amazingly high percentage of World War I deaths were related to the use of gas."

6c. *Word(s) Omitted from the Middle of a Sentence*

Delete the word(s) chosen for omission and connect the remaining parts of the sentence with three spaced dots (with no space before or after them) as shown with the single omission (example 2) and the multiple omissions (example 3).

Examples

1. *Original Quotation:* "I firmly believe that a statistical analysis will show that an amazingly high percentage of World War I deaths were related to the use of gas."
2. *Single Omission*: "I firmly believe…an amazingly high percentage of World War I deaths were related to the use of gas."
3. *Multiple Omissions*: "I…believe…an amazingly high percentage of World War I deaths were related to…gas."

6d. Word(s) Omitted from the End of a Sentence

Delete the words chosen for omission. Move the end punctuation (period, question mark, or exclamation point) of the original sentence so that it becomes the standard-spaced end punctuation of the newly created shortened sentence. Place three spaced ellipsis dots and closing quotation marks after the end punctuation. The procedure is the same whether the sentence ends with a period (example 1) a question mark (example 2), or an exclamation point (example 3).

Examples

1. *Original Quotation*: "An unusually high number of soldiers were killed in World War I because of the use of gas by both sides."
   After the Omission: "An unusually high number of soldiers were killed in World War I because of the use of gas…."

2. *Original Quotation:* "Were an unusually high number of soldiers killed in World War I because of the use of gas by both sides?"
   After the Omission: "Were an unusually high number of soldiers killed in World War I because of the use of gas?…"
3. *Original Quotation:* "An unusually high number of soldiers died in World War I because of the use of gas by both sides!"
   After the Omission: "An unusually high number of soldiers were killed in World War I because of the use of gas!…"

6e. *Sentence Ending with an Omission and a Source Citation*

The APA (examples 1-3) source citation (author, year, page) follows the traditional ellipsis mark, three spaced dots (…). The MLA (examples 4-6) citation (author, page) follows an ellipsis mark whose three spaced dots are enclosed in brackets ([…]).

In either case, a period is always placed after the parentheses enclosing a source citation at the end of a sentence. When the omission occurs at the end of a sentence concluded with a period, leave the accompanying ellipsis (three spaced dots) and closing quotation marks, and put the period after the source citation parentheses (examples 1, 4). The procedure is the same after placing question marks (examples 2, 5) and exclamation points (examples 3, 6)

Examples

1. "An unusually high number of soldiers were killed..." (Doe, 1998, p.67).
2. "Were an unusually high number of soldiers killed?..." (Doe, 1998, p. 67).
3. "An unbelievably high number of soldiers were killed!..." (Doe, 1998, p. 67).
4. "An unusually high number of soldiers were killed [...]" (Doe 67).
5. "Were an unusually high number of soldiers killed? [...]" (Doe 67).
6. "An unbelievably high number of soldiers were killed! [...]" (Doe 67).

6f. Omission of Sentence(s)

Place three spaced dots after the end punctuation (period, question mark, exclamation point) of the last complete sentence before the omission (example 2).

Examples

1. *Original Quotation*: "There were an unusually high number of soldiers killed in World War I. Following the war, scholars considered many possible reasons for the high mortality rate. Most historians now attribute the high death rate to the extensive use of gas by armies on both sides."
2. *After the Omission*: "There were an unusually high number of soldiers killed in World War I.... Most historians attribute the high death rate to the extensive use of gas by armies on both sides."

6g. *Omission of Paragraphs(s)*

Place three spaced dots after the end punctuation of the last complete sentence before the omission (example 2). The first word in each succeeding paragraph after the omission is preceded by quotation marks and begins with a capital letter. Closing quotation marks are only placed after the end punctuation of the final paragraph in the quotation.

Examples

1. *Original Quotation*: "XYZ Company held its annual meeting at the Hobogoblin Hotel in March. Sales were flat then, and the board of directors was asked to move quickly to correct the situation.

   "John Doe, board chairman, introduced a number of ideas for turning the company around. Changes in accounting and public relations headed his list of proposals.

   "Now seven months later, the company is headed toward its most profitable year ever. This just shows what can happen when we all pull together."

2. *After the Omission*: "XYZ Company held its annual meeting at the Hoboglobin Hotel in March. Sales were flat then, and the board of directors was asked to move quickly to correct the situation....

   "Now seven months later, the company is headed toward its most profitable year ever. This just shows what can happen when we all pull together."

6h. *Ellipsis Dots and Poetry*

Poetry of three lines or less may be presented in regular text with the use of the slash (/). The first line begins with quotation marks and a capital letter. All lines are presented as originally written (same capitalization, punctuation, etc.). Lines are separated by a slash, with one space on either side. The end of the last line is followed with punctuation, as appropriate, and closing quotation marks (example 1).

When there are more than three lines, (example 2), poetry is introduced with a colon, displayed in block form without quotation marks, and indented (ten spaces from the left margin for MLA).

Words at the end of a line that would otherwise extend beyond the right-hand margin are carried over to the next line, which is indented an additional three spaces.

Omissions of one or more lines (lines 5 and 6 in example 3), are indicated by a line of spaced dots (enclosed in brackets [...] for MLA style). If there is a source citation, it follows the last line, and it is free standing (example 3).

Examples

1. The first three lines of that poem are "There once was a man from Boston / Who regularly dreamed dreams but lost them; / Until one morning something occurred quite profound."
2. The complete poem is as follows:
>   There once was a man from Boston
>   Who regularly dreamed dreams but lost
>   them;

> Until one morning something occurred quite profound
> And the dreams usually lost, he finally found!

3. With the fourth and fifth lines deleted, the poem would be presented this way:

> There once was a man from Boston
> Who regularly dreamed dreams but lost them;
> --
> And the dreams usually lost, he finally found! (Doe 697)

6i. *Ellipsis Dots after an Unfinished Sentence*

Three spaced ellipsis dots may conclude an unfinished sentence when its meaning is clear, and the original speaker or writer intentionally left it incomplete. The unfinished sentence may be a quote (example 1) or regular copy (example 2). *NOTE*: Do not confuse the use of ellipsis dots at the end of an unfinished sentence with their use to indicate the deletion of material from the end of a quoted complete sentence. In the latter instance, when words are deleted from the end of a complete sentence, the new shortened sentence concludes with its original end punctuation, ellipsis dots, and quotation marks. (See "Word(s) Omitted from the End of a Sentence," page 24.)

<u>Examples</u>

1. John said, "If it tastes good, you just know some medical study will claim it has too many calories, too much fat, not enough…"

2. If it tastes good, you just know some medical study will claim it has too many calories, too much fat, not enough fiber...

7. *Long Quotation Formats: Block or Rolling*

A long quotation, one of forty words or more, may be presented in either of two formats: Block or Rolling.

7a. *Block Format*

In block format, the quoted text is heavily indented to create a freestanding block that has no opening or closing quotation marks. Between-the-lines spacing in the quoted paragraph(s) should be the same as that used in the regular text.

When using block format, begin by placing a colon after the introducing attribution (he said: / she said:) or after the introducing sentence.

Start on a new line and arrange the quotation into a freestanding block by indenting each of its lines ten spaces from the left margin for MLA format (example 1) and five spaces from the left margin for APA style. Maintain the same right-hand margin for both the block quotation and the regular text.

In MLA format, if the block quotation is two or more paragraphs, indent the first line of <u>each</u> paragraph (including the first) an additional three spaces (example 2).

In APA format, if the block quotation is two or more paragraphs, maintain the first paragraph as an unindented block. But indent the first line of each succeeding paragraph an additional five spaces (example 3).

With both formats, if a source citation is needed, place it in freestanding parentheses outside the end punctuation of the final (or only) paragraph in the block quotation. See (*) in example 3. There is no punctuation after the parentheses.

The first line of regular text immediately following a block quotation is indented five spaces if it begins a new paragraph (examples 2, 3).

<u>Examples</u>

1. (MLA)

    During the morning board of directors meeting, President John Doe said:

    >The company plans to_____
    >_____.
    >Phase I will_____
    >_____.

    The meeting concluded with_____
    _____.

2. (MLA)

    During the morning board of directors meeting, President John Doe said:

    >The company plans to_____
    >_____.
    >Phase I will_____.
    >In the middle years, two or three buildings_____.
    >Finally, we will_____
    >_____.

    In the afternoon session, the board_____
    _____.

3. (APA)
During the morning board of directors meeting, President John Doe said:

The company plans to _____.
Phase I will _____.
In the middle years, two or three buildings _____.
Finally, we will _____
_____.
In the afternoon session, the board_____
_____.(*)

7b. *Rolling Format*

With many types of writing (e.g., newspaper, magazine, journal articles, lengthy dialogue, etc.), it is common for authors to "roll" long quotations into standard paragraphs.

In rolling format, the attribution (he said/she said) is usually followed by a comma.

Each paragraph begins with quotation marks and a capital letter.

Each paragraph except the final one concludes with the appropriate end punctuation (e.g., period, question mark, or exclamation point) but without closing quotation marks.

The final paragraph concludes with the proper end punctuation and closing quotation marks. If a source citation is needed, place it in parentheses followed by a period.*

Example

During the morning board of directors meeting, President John Doe said, "The company plans to_____. Phase I will_____.

"In the middle years, two or three buildings _____

_____.

"Finally, we will_____

_____."

OR

"Finally, we will_____

_____"(*).

8. *Dialogue*

Paragraphing is the grammatical cue which keeps readers informed when dialogue is used. With dialogue, the writer must begin a new paragraph each time a new speaker is introduced and each time there is a change in speakers. In literature, dialogue can be either Exterior or Interior.

8a. *Exterior Dialogue*

Exterior dialogue is the external conversation that takes place between two or more individuals. Generally, the identity of each speaker is first established through the use of a he said/she said attribution (examples 1-3). Later in the dialogue, the he said/she said attributions may be interspersed with or replaced by more subtle methods of identifying speakers.

These methods include presenting speakers in the same rotating order (examples 4-6), placing self-identifying information in a comment ("a close friend like me," example 6), or having a speaker use a word or phrase already established earlier in the dialogue as unique to him or her ("Darling," examples 2,5).

When the dialogue for a single speaker runs longer than one paragraph (examples 6, 7), begin each succeeding paragraph with opening quotation marks and a capital letter. But place closing quotation marks only after the end punctuation of the last paragraph.

Examples

1. "You ought to listen to me," said George. "After all, I am your husband, and I know what looks best on you."

2. "Darling, you are my husband, but you are still a man and sometimes a woman has a better perspective on what looks good on another woman," answered Margaret.

3. "Yes, as a woman and Margaret's best friend, I think I may well have a better idea about what looks best on her than any man, even a very attentive husband," agreed Janice.

4. "Maybe so, but I'm a guy, and I know what looks good to us."

5. "Thank you, Darling, but you may be just a little too loyal for my own good."

6. "That is so right. Many men do let their love or loyalty for the women in their lives affect their objectivity. They either can't see it or

won't admit it when a woman they care about seems to want to wear something that really won't be becoming to her. However, another woman, especially a close friend like me, is in a position to be more objective.

7. "For instance, no matter how attractive a woman is, unless she is also very slender, a bikini bathing suit is not likely to be the most flattering style she could choose. A man may not be able to say that to a woman he cares about, but another woman usually will."

8b. *Dashes with Dialogue*

The dash is typed as two hyphens with no space between it and the text that precedes or follows it. When a speaker is interrupted, indecisive, hesitant, evasive, or confused, end an unfinished quotation with a dash placed inside its closing quote marks. Add no other punctuation regardless of whether the sentence- -had it been completed- -would have been a statement (examples 1,2), a question (examples 3,4) or an exclamation (examples 5,6).

Examples

1. "Just because I love you doesn't mean that you- -" she mumbled through her tears.
2. She mumbled through her tears, "Just because I love you doesn't mean that you- -"
3. "Wouldn't it be better if first I- -" he started to ask.
4. He started to ask, "Wouldn't it be better if first I- -"

5. "Turn the wheel before that truck- -" he screamed out in terror.
6. Bob screamed out in terror, "Turn the wheel before that truck- -"

8c. *Ellipsis as an Alternative for the Dash*

As an alternative for the dash, three spaced dots (periods) may be used at the end of a quotation to indicate that the speaker has been interrupted or to reflect that the speaker is indecisive, hesitant, evasive, or confused (examples 2, 4).

<u>Examples</u>

1. "Sue, I really want you to- -" he started to say.
2. "Sue, I really want you to…" he started to say.
3. He started to say, "Sue, I really want you to- -"
4. He started to say, "Sue, I really want you to…"

8d. *Interior Dialogue*

Interior dialogue is the internal conversation that takes place entirely within a single individual's mind. It includes private thoughts and comments imagined as speech but not actually spoken to anyone else.

Interior dialogue can be punctuated like exterior dialogue by using a combination of commas and quotation marks (examples 1-3). It can also be punctuated using only commas and without quotation marks (examples 4,5). When only commas are used, capitalizing the first word of interior dialogue is optional (example 4), although it usually is (example 5). Whichever the choice, its use should be consistent throughout the same work.

<u>Examples</u>

1. "I'll go to the store," thought George, "and get the rat poison we need."
2. As he watched the helicopter crash to earth, Bob said to himself, "There is no chance that anyone can survive that!"
3. I guess I should have said, "You know that I really do deserve to get a bigger raise."
4. As he watched the helicopter crash to earth, he said to himself, there is no chance that anyone can survive that!
5. As he watched the helicopter crash to earth, he said to himself, There is no chance that anyone can survive that!

9. *When Quotations Are Not Preceded by a Comma*

A quoted sentence is ordinarily separated from its words of attribution (he said/she said, etc.) by a comma. But there are three notable exceptions. In general, a comma is not used when the quotation comes after a linking verb, follows a gerund (*-ing* verbal) that is the noun object of a stated or unstated preposition, or comes after an infinitive that includes a verb of speaking or writing. The standard rules for capitalization apply. Unless preceded by the word *that*, a quoted sentence begins with a capital letter (examples 1, 3, 5, 7). A quoted fragment is all lowercase (examples 2, 4, 6, 8) unless it contains proper nouns or begins a sentence.

9a. *After a Linking Verb*

Generally, a quotation following a linking verb is not preceded by a comma. Linking verbs include all of the forms of the verb *be* (am, are, be, been, being, is, was, were); verbs of the five senses- -see, hear, touch, taste, smell; and other verbs that express condition, such as appear, became, become, feel, grow, look, remain, sound, etc.

Examples

1. Allan's comment <u>was</u> "Too many cooks spoil the broth."
2. Allan's comment <u>was</u> "too many cooks."

9b. *After Gerund Object of Preposition*

Generally, a quotation following a gerund (*-ing* verbal) that is the noun object of a stated or unstated preposition is not preceded by a comma. The gerund *saying* is the object of the preposition *by* in examples 3 and 4. *By* is unstated but understood in examples 5 and 6.

Examples

3. Allan ended the conversation <u>*by* saying</u> "Too many cooks spoil the broth."
4. Allan ended the conversation *by* <u>saying</u> "too many cooks."
5. Allan ended the conversation <u>saying</u> "Too many cooks spoil the broth."
6. Allan ended the conversation <u>saying</u> "too many cooks."

9c. *After an Infinitive*

Generally, a quotation following an infinitive that includes a verb of speaking or writing is not preceded by a comma.

Examples

7. Allan loved to proclaim "Too many cooks spoil the broth."
8. Allan loved to proclaim "too many cooks."

9d. *Exception to the Exceptions*

In dialogue, the attributing words are always separated from their quotation (usually by comma) even when the quotation follows a linking verb (examples 9, 10), a gerund object of a stated or unstated preposition (examples 11-14), or an infinitive that includes a verb of speaking or writing (examples 15, 16).

With dialogue, the quotation begins with a capital letter whether it is a complete sentence or a fragment.

Examples

9. Allan's comment was, "Too many cooks spoil the broth."
10. Allan's comment was, "Too many cooks."
11. Allan ended the conversation by saying, "Too many cooks spoil the broth."
12. Allan ended the conversation by saying, "Too many cooks."
13. Allan ended the conversation saying, "Too many cooks spoil the broth."

14. Allan ended the conversation saying, "Too many cooks."
15. Allan loved to proclaim, "Too many cooks spoil the broth."
16. Allan loved to proclaim, "Too many cooks."

10. *Adages, Axioms, Maxims, Mottoes, Proverbs, Rules, Sayings, Truisms*

The rules for handling adages, axioms, maxims, mottoes, proverbs, rules, sayings, and truisms are the same. For the purposes of this discussion, the term *adage* will represent all of them.

Adages begin with a capital letter except when introduced by the word *that*. Set off with quotation marks or not, an adage preceded by *that* begins with a lowercase letter unless its own first word is a proper noun. There is no comma before or after *that* (examples 1, 2)

At the writer's option, an adage may be set off with a comma and quotation marks (example 3); set off with quotation marks but no comma (example 4); set off with a comma but no quotation marks (example 5); or presented without a comma or quotation marks (example 6). Whichever the choice, its use should be consistent throughout the same work.

Examples

1. The first rule is_that_"a penny saved is a penny earned."
2. The first rule is_that_a penny saved is a penny earned.

3. The first rule is, "A penny saved is a penny earned."
4. The first rule is_"A penny saved is a penny earned."
5. The first rule is, A penny saved is a penny earned.
6. The first rule is_A penny saved is a penny earned.

10a. Hints for Handling Adages That Are Appositives

Appositives that follow a noun introduced by an indefinite article (*a* or *an*) are usually nonrestrictive and set off with commas (example 1). Appositives that follow a noun introduced by the definite article *the* are usually restrictive and not set off with commas (example 2).

Examples

1. An old adage, "A penny saved is a penny earned," appeals to almost everyone.
2. The old adage_"A penny saved is a penny earned_" appeals to almost everyone.

11. Freestanding Epigrams, Epigraphs and Quotations

Freestanding epigrams, epigraphs, and quotations may be heavily indented, centered, placed above the text, or set off in other ways.

The attribution is preceded by a dash and may consist of the author alone, the author and source, or the source of the work by itself. Either a comma (examples 1, 3) or a colon (examples 2, 4) may be used between the author and the original source of the work displayed. When the source is provided, it should be underlined (examples 1, 2), displayed in italics (examples 3, 4), or placed within quotation marks (example 5), as grammatically appropriate. No punctuation is placed after a freestanding attribution (examples 1–9)

Examples

1. "Oh, what a great big jelly bean ride."- -John Doe, <u>Doe Diaries</u>
2. Oh, what a great big jell bean ride.- -John Doe: <u>Doe Diaries</u>
3. "Oh, what a great big jelly bean ride."- -John Doe, *Doe Diaries*
4. Oh, what a great big jelly bean ride.- -John Doe: *Doe Diaries*
5. "The big jelly bean always wins"- -John Doe, "Doe Sketches"
6. "No wampum means no house, no car, no food, no fun."- -Author Unknown
7. No wampum means no house, no car, no food, no fun.- -Author Unknown
8. "No wampum means no house, no car, no food, no fun."   - -Author Unknown
9. No wampum means no house, no car, no food, no fun.   - -Author Unknown

12. *Indirect Quotation*

An indirect quotation is not a quotation. It is a restatement that presents the same information as a quotation but in different words. Recall that a quotation is an exact reproduction of the word(s) originally spoken or written by someone else.

In contrast, an indirect quotation is a statement about (examples 1, 2, 3, 4) or a report of (examples 5, 6) the word(s) originally spoken or written by someone else.

An indirect quotation begins with a lowercase letter and is not set off by commas or by quotation marks. It is often introduced by the word *that* (example 3) or by a subordinating conjunction (examples 1, 2, and 4). Like adverbs, subordinating conjunctions are words that indicate when, where, why, how, or how much. Frequently used subordinating conjunctions include although, after, as if, even if, if, as long as, because, before, even though, now that, once, rather than, so that, since, then, though, till, unless, until, what, whereas, whether, whenever, wherever, etc.

Examples

Original Quotations

A. "Will you please help me?" he asked. (See examples 1, 2, 4.)
B. John says, "An amazingly high percentage of World War I deaths were related to the use of gas." (See example 3)
C. John explained, "Sue, you have to go home right now." (See examples 5, 6.)

Indirect Quotations

1. He asked <u>whether</u> I would help him.
2. He asked <u>if</u> I would help him.
3. John said <u>that</u> an amazingly high number of soldiers died in World War I because of the use of gas.

4. <u>Because</u> gas was used, according to John, the number of World War I deaths was abnormally high.
5. John said Sue had to go home right away.
6. John told Sue she had to go home immediately.

COMMAS

The comma is arguably the most frequently used mark of punctuation in the English language. Paradoxically, it may also be the most overused and the most underused. Without question, the comma is the most misused and the most misunderstood of the grammatical symbols.

Whenever possible, comma use should be closely governed by the traditional guidelines and standard rules long established through usage. However, punctuation is not an exact science nor are its rules all inclusive. On rare occasions, for reasons of nuance or to prevent misinterpretation, a comma not otherwise called for may be warranted. In such instances, comma use is a matter of writer discretion.

13. *Commas with Absolute Phrases*

An absolute phrase consists of a noun or pronoun, a stated or understood participle (*ing-* or *ed-* ending verbal), and any modifiers.

As independent elements that modify the whole sentence rather than any particular part of it, absolute phrases are always set off, usually by comma(s).

Examples

1. <u>The tide having moved in so quickly</u>, Jerry had little time to reach safety.
2. Jerry will have little time, <u>the tide already sweeping across the jetty</u>, to safely reach shore.
3. <u>Massive storm clouds ahead and behind</u>, the small vessel seemed doomed. (The participle *being* [...clouds being ahead and behind] is understood.)
4. Their young audience in a rage, promoters offered full refunds to disappointed ticket buyers. (The participle *being* [...audience being in a rage] is understood.)

14. **A, An, The** *as Adjectives in a Series*

In a series, the three articles (*a, an, the*) are always noncoordinate adjectives and are never separated from a following adjective by a comma (e.g., a_big, red, bent section).

15. *No Comma Before the First Adjective in a Series*

Never place a comma before the first adjective in a series (e.g., _young, slender girl)

16. *No Comma after the Final Adjective in a Series*

Never place a comma after the final adjective in a series (e.g., young, slender_girl).

17. *Numbers as Adjectives in a Series*

In a series, numbers are always noncoordinate adjectives and are never separated from a following adjective by a comma (e.g., three_big, red, bent sections; 125_ big, red, bent sections).

18. *Commas with Addresses*

With an address, place commas before and after each item after the first. There is no comma between the state and a ZIP code (example 2).

Examples

1. This load must be delivered to the 228 Charlotte Street, Manakin, Virginia, address by midnight.
2. Mail this to 228 Charlotte Street, Manakin, VA 23103, by midnight Tuesday.

19. *Commas with Direct Address*

Use a comma or commas to set off words of direct address regardless of their position within a sentence (examples 1-3)

Examples

1. George, I need you to help me.
2. I need you to help me, George.
3. Next month, my good friends, I will be a commissioned officer.

20. *Commas with Adverbial Clauses*

An adverbial clause, which consists of an introductory adverb (word that indicates when, where, why, how, or how much), a subject, verb, and any modifiers, is set off by a comma when it comes *before* the subject of a sentence (example 1). As a general rule, adverb clauses that come *after* the subject of a sentence are not set off (example 2).

Examples

1. Because he eats so much greasy food, George fears his cholesterol level is too high.
2. George fears his cholesterol level is too high because he eats so much greasy food.

21. *Commas with* As, Since

Use commas before the subordinating conjunctions *as* (example 1) or *since* (example 2) when they mean *"because."*

Examples

1. Fine restaurants are economically important to the inner city, *as* they attract paying customers to the downtown area.
2. John wants to do something special for his mother, *since* today is her birthday.

22. *Commas for Clarity*

Use a comma between sentence elements that could be misunderstood (example 1) or would be nonsensical without it (example 2).

Examples

1. In 1900, 8,000 people in Galveston, Texas, died from a hurricane.
2. After eating, the players all went back to the hotel.

23. *Commas When Compound Subject has Positive and Negative Elements*

In a compound subject where one subject is positive and one is negative, the negative subject is set off with commas. The verb, singular (example 1) or plural (example 2), always agrees with the positive subject.

<u>Examples</u>

1. <u>David</u>, not the Ross brothers, <u>is</u> the one who deserves the credit.
2. The Ross <u>brothers</u>, not David, <u>are</u> the ones who deserve the credit.

24. *Commas, Conjunctions, and Compound Items in a Series*

In a series punctuated by commas, it is correct to include the final comma before a conjunction that precedes the last item (example 1). It is also correct to omit the final series comma before the conjunction when there is no likelihood of misinterpretation (example 2).

Parts of a compound term (e.g., "bacon and eggs" in example 3) are not separated by comma.

If the final two items in a series are to be understood as a single, combined entity (e.g., "hostess and manager" in example 4), they are not separated by comma.

If the final two items in a series are to be seen as separate entities (example 5), they are separated by comma.

Examples

1. My favorite birds are owls, hawks, and crows.
2. My favorite birds are owls, hawks_and crows.
3. The menu included coffee, pancakes, <u>bacon and eggs</u>, toast, milk and cereal.
4. The restaurant ad lists several job openings: valet, cook, busboy, hostess_and manager.
5. The restaurant ad lists several job openings: valet, cook, busboy, hostess, and manager.

25. *Comma Use before a Concluding Dependent Clause*

If a concluding dependent clause introduces a new idea, it should be preceded by a comma (example 1). However, if a concluding dependent clause merely adds to or continues the thought already presented in the main clause, no comma is used (example 2).

Examples

1. He bailed Doug of out jail, although they are not related.
2. We would have had a big turnout_if only half of the people we invited attended.

26. *Commas with Contrasting Elements*

Use commas to set off contrasting coordinate elements (example 1) and expressions introduced by <u>not</u>, <u>but not</u>, <u>though not</u>, etc. (example 2).

Examples

1. Termites do their damage quietly, yet effectively.
2. It was John Doe, not the butler, who did it.

27. *Commas with Coordinating Conjunctions* (Fan Boys)

There are seven coordinating conjunctions, easily remembered by the acronym *fan boys* (for, and, nor, but, or, yet, so). When there are complete sentences (independent clauses) on both sides of a coordinating conjunction, the conjunction must be preceded by a comma (example 1). Otherwise, unless it is part of a series or a parenthetic expression, a coordinating conjunction is not preceded by a comma (example 2).

If either or both of two sentences joined by a coordinating conjunction have internal commas, the comma that would otherwise precede the conjunction is replaced by a semicolon (example 3).

Examples

1. Jack wanted 40 candles on the cake, but he got only three.
2. Jack wanted 40 candles_but got only three. (But connects a complete sentence with a phrase)
3. Jack, my best friend, wanted 40 candles on the cake; but he got only three.

28. *Commas with Dates*

When the day, month, and year are given, place commas before and after each item after the first (examples 1, 2).

When only the month and day (when the day is a number) are given, no commas are used (examples 3, 4).

When the day of the week is combined with the numerical day and its month, the latter is set off with commas (examples 5, 6).

When only the month and year are given, commas are optional (examples 7, 8).

Commas are not used when parts of a date are joined by a preposition (example 9) or when the day date is placed before the month (example 10).

Examples

1. August 5, 2005, is when the contract expires.
2. The town's newest bank opened on Tuesday, May 18, 2002, with a big ceremony.
3. September 20 is the final deadline.
4. The September 20 deadline is fast approaching.
5. Sunday, June 5, is when he will graduate.
6. Graduation is scheduled for Sunday, June 5, in the auditorium
7. John was born in March, 2002, in Detroit.
8. John was born in March_2002_in Detroit.
9. John was born in March of 2002 in Detroit.
10. John was born on 18 March 2002 in Detroit.

29. *Commas with Degrees and Titles*

When they come after a name, place commas before and after a degree or title (examples 1, 2). Commas with Jr., Sr., IV, etc., are optional (examples 3, 4)

Examples

1. John Smith, M.A., is the new agency director.
2. John Smith, police chief, is this month's speaker.
3. John Smith, Sr., is the new company president.
4. John Smith_Sr._ is the new company president.

30. Commas with Infinitive Phrases

An infinitive phrase, which consists of the word *to*, a verb, and any words closely related to it, is set off by comma when it comes <u>before</u> the subject of a sentence (example 1). As a general rule, infinitive phrases that come <u>after</u> the subject of a sentence are not set off (example 2).

<u>Examples</u>

1. To get a driver's license in Virginia, Jack has to pass a written test.
2. Jack has to pass a written test to get a driver's license in Virginia.

31. Commas with Participial Phrases

A participial phrase, which consists of an *-ing* or *-ed* ending verb and any modifiers, is set off by comma when it comes <u>before</u> the subject of a sentence (examples 1, 3). As a general rule, participial phrases that come <u>after</u> the subject of a sentence are not set off (examples 2, 4).

<u>Examples</u>

1. <u>Hoping</u> for adventure, my friends set out in their brand new canoe.
2. My friends set out in their brand new canoe <u>hoping</u> for adventure.
3. <u>Devastated</u> by the events of the day, Bill left the crash site.
4. Bill left the crash site <u>devastated</u> by the events of the day.

32. *Commas with Prepositional Phrases*

Place a comma after a long introductory prepositional phrase (five or more words) or after a series of two or more short ones when they come <u>before</u> the subject of a sentence (examples 1, 3). As a general rule, prepositional phrases that come <u>after</u> the subject of a sentence are not set off (examples 2, 4).

<u>Examples</u>

1. In that big, brightly colored basket, John found a huge poisonous snake.
2. John found a huge poisonous snake_in that big, brightly colored basket.
3. On a clear day in the spring, one can see the city from here.
4. One can see the city from here_on a clear day in the spring.

33. *Commas with Place Names*

With a place name, put commas before and after each item after the first.

<u>Example</u>

Saratoga Springs, New York, is the family's vacation destination.

34. *Series Using Only Commas*

Conjunctions may be omitted if commas are used between all the items in a series (e.g., cars, trucks, boats, planes).

35. Series Using Only Conjunctions

Commas may be omitted if conjunctions (and, or, etc.) are used between all the items in a series (e.g., cars *and* trucks *and* boats *and* planes).

36. Series of Names in a Firm's Title

Unless specified by the firm itself, do not place a comma before *and* in a series of names that forms a firm's title (e.g., King, Layton, Ambrose, Rucker_ and Colston).

37. Never Place Commas after **Such As** or **Like**

Never place a comma or other punctuation (e.g., colon, etc.) immediately after the preposition *like* or the term *such as*. Never use commas to set off a phrase introduced by *like* or *such as* when it is restrictive and essential to the meaning of the sentence (example 1, 3). However, when it is nonrestrictive, place a comma in front of *like* or *such as* and after the phrase introduced (examples 2, 4). If a nonrestrictive phrase ends the sentence, its concluding comma is replaced by a period or other appropriate end punctuation (example 5).

<u>Examples</u>

1. Inventors_*like* Thomas Edison_have changed the course of history.
2. Alexander Graham Bell, *like* Thomas Edison, was an inventor who changed the course of history.
3. Foods_ *such as* hamburgers and French fries_ have a high concentration of fat.

4. Foods with a high concentration of fat, *such as* hamburgers and French fries, should be balanced with fruits and vegetables to achieve a healthy diet.
   5. To achieve a healthy diet, fruits and vegetables should be added to meals that would otherwise consists of only foods high in fat, such as hamburgers and French fries<u>.</u>

38. *Commas with Social Salutation and Close*

Use a comma after the salutation (e.g., Dear Sue,) and after the close of a social or personal letter (e.g., Cordially, With love, etc.).

39. *Commas with a Tag Question*

Place a comma between a statement and the brief question that follows it when the subject of the statement and the subject of the question is the same entity (example 1). When they have different subjects, the statement and the question must be punctuated as separate grammatical elements (example 2).

Examples
   1. <u>George</u> was not there, was <u>he</u>?
   2. <u>I</u> will never stay in that hotel again<u>.</u> Will <u>you</u>?

40. *Comma When* **That** *Is Understood*

A comma may be used in place of the word *that* when its presence as a conjunction is understood but not stated (example 2).

Examples

1. The fall is stock prices came so quickly *that* the small investor had almost no time to react.
2. The fall in stock prices came so quickly, the small investor had almost no time to react.

41. *Commas to Set Off Transposed Modifiers*

When adjectives or adverbs that might normally be expected to come before the word(s) they modify (example 1) are instead placed after them for dramatic effect, they are said to have been transposed. Transposed modifiers are always set off by commas (example 2).

Examples

1. Jack was always a pleasant, happy, and smiling child.
2. Jack was always a pleasant child, happy and smiling.

42. *Comma in Place of Word(s) Omitted*

If through parallel construction or context the meaning is clear, a word or words used in the first clause of a compound sentence may be omitted and merely understood in its other clause(s). In such instances, a comma is used in place of the deleted word(s), marking the location of the omission(s) (example 2).

Examples

1. David was born in Spartanburg, Kerry was born in Washington, and Rosanne was born in Charlotte.
2. David was born in Spartanburg, Kerry, in Washington, and Rosanne, in Charlotte. (Commas mark the omissions of <u>was</u> <u>born</u> in the second and third clauses.)

43. *Commas with Words, Phrases, or Clauses in a Series*

Use commas when there are three or more words (example 1), phrases (example 2), dependent clauses, (example 3), or independent clauses (example 4) in a series.

Examples

1. The baseball coach issued uniforms, helmets, and gloves.
2. They placed ads on the internet, on radio, and on television.
3. The detective wanted to know who had access to the building, where the safe was located, and when the theft occurred.
4. They had the desire, they had the discipline, and they had the knowledge necessary to succeed.

44. *Commas with Yes, No, and Other Responses*

Use a comma to set off *yes, no,* and other similar responses. For more emphasis, an exclamation point may replace the comma (examples 3, 4, 6).

The use of a capital letter after an exclamation point is not required, but it is an option (example 4).

Examples

1. *No,* I don't want to go that late.
2. *Okay,* let's all go right now.
3. *Okay!* let's all go right now.
4. *Okay!* Let's all go right now.
5. *Oh,* I really didn't mean that.
6. *Oh!* I really didn't mean that.

45. *Direct Question*

A directly stated question (simply question, hereafter) always concludes with a question mark immediately behind it whether it is positioned at the beginning, in the middle, or at the end of a sentence (examples 1-5).

A question that starts a sentence (example 1) or a stand-alone question (example 6) must begin with a capital letter.

The use of a capital letter to begin a question introduced after another part of a sentence (examples 2, 4, 7, 9, 11) or to begin each question in a series (example 13) is a matter of emphasis and is optional, although capital letters are generally preferred. Whichever the choice, its use should be consistent throughout the same work.

A question should not be placed in quotation marks unless it is part of an existing quotation.

A question may be introduced by comma (examples 2-5); by colon (examples 7, 8); by semicolon (examples 9, 10); or by dash (examples 11, 12).

Questions in a series may be separated by commas and concluded by a single question mark. When commas are used, each question after the first begins with a lowercase letter (example 15).

Examples:

1. Is that really gold? they wonder.
2. They wonder, Is that really gold? every time they see it.
3. They wonder, is that really gold? every time they see it.
4. They wonder, Is that really gold?
5. They wonder, is that really gold?
6. Is that really gold?
7. The board had one question: Is that really gold?
8. The board had one question: is that really gold?
9. The board had one question; Is that really gold?
10. The board had one question; is that really gold?
11. The board had one question- -Is that really gold?
12. The board had one question- -is that really gold?
13. Is that bracelet made of gold? An imitation metal? A metallic-coated plastic?
14. Is that bracelet made of gold? an imitation metal? a metallic-coated plastic?
15. Is that bracelet made of gold, an imitation metal, a metallic-coated plastic?

46. *Question Mark in Brackets or Parentheses to Express Doubt*

Within quoted copy, place a question mark enclosed in brackets behind a date, fact, or number whose historical accuracy is in doubt (examples 1-3).

Within regular copy, place a question mark enclosed in parentheses behind a date, fact, or number whose historical accuracy is in doubt (examples 4-6).

Examples

1. She said, "Many historians believe John Doe was born in 1620 [?]."
2. She said, "Many historians believe John Doe was born in London [?]."
3. She said, "Many historians believe John Doe had six [?] children."
4. John Doe was born in 1620 (?).
5. John Doe was born in London (?).
6. John Doe has six (?) children.

47. *Abbreviation c. Before a Date That Is in Doubt*

As an alternative to the question mark, place *c.*, the abbreviation for *circa* (Latin for *about*), before a date whose historical accuracy is in doubt (example). The abbreviation c. is only applicable with dates and may not be used before facts or numbers.

Example

John Doe was born c. 1620.

48. *Indirect Question*

An indirect question is not a question. It is a restatement that presents the same information as the question but in different words. Recall that a direct question always ends with a question mark.

In contrast, an indirect question is a statement about a direct question, and it ends with a period.

An indirect question begins with a lowercase letter and is not set off by comma(s), quotation marks, or other punctuation.

An indirect question is often introduced by the word *that* (example 2) or by a subordinating conjunction (examples 1, 3).

Like adverbs, subordinating conjunctions are words that indicate when, where, why, how, or how much. Frequently used subordinating conjunctions include although, after, as if, even if, if, as long as, because, before, even though, now that, once, rather than, so that, since, then, though, till, unless, until, what, whereas, whether, when, where, while, whenever, wherever, etc.

Examples

Original Direct Question
"Shouldn't you go right now and help?" Bob asked.

Indirect Question
1. Bob asked <u>if</u> I would go and help.
2. Bob asked <u>that</u> I go and help.
3. Bob asked <u>whether</u> I would go and help.

49. *Correcting Comma Splices and Run-on Sentences*

A comma splice is created when two complete sentences (independent clauses) are joined together using only a comma between them (e.g., Virginia is an excellent student, she enjoys all types of music).

A run-on (fused) sentence results when two complete sentences are joined together with no punctuation between them (e.g., Virginia is an excellent student_she enjoys all types of music).

The six methods available to correct these errors are the same whether the problem is a comma splice or a run-on sentence (examples 1-7).

49a. Correct by Creating Two Separate Sentences

Example

1. Virginia is an excellent student. She enjoys all types of music.

49b. Correct with a Semicolon

Example

2. Virginia is an excellent student; she enjoys all types of music.

49c. Correct with a Colon

A colon may be used to join two sentences if the second sentence explains or expands on information provided by the first.

Example

3. Virginia is an excellent student: she won a full scholarship.

49d. Correct by Subordinating an Independent Clause

Placing a subordinating conjunction (*because*, in example) before an independent clause makes it dependent. An introductory dependent clause is set off by comma. (Subordinating conjunctions are discussed in section 48, "Indirect Question," on pages 61, 62.)

Example

4. *Because* Virginia is an excellent student, she won a full scholarship.

49e. *Correct with a Semicolon, Conjunctive Adverb, and Comma*

Example

5. Virginia is an excellent student; *consequently*, she won a full scholarship.

49f. *Correct with a Comma and Coordinating Conjunction*

There are seven coordinating conjunctions. Remember them as the acronym *fan boys*- -for, and, nor, but, or, yet, so (example 6). If there is an internal comma in either or both sentences, a semicolon replaces the comma before the coordinating conjunction (example 7).

Example

6. Virginia is an excellent student, *and* she won a full scholarship.
7. Virginia is an excellent student; and in her senior year, she won a full scholarship.

50. *Rarely Used Comma Options*

In the rare instance when two or more very short independent clauses have the same subject and are very similar in form, they may be separated using only commas (example 1) or only semicolons (example 2). There is always the option to punctuate them as separate sentences (example 3).

Examples

1. We came, we saw, we conquered.
2. We came; we saw; we conquered.
3. We came. We saw. We conquered.

51. *Pairings Testing to Punctuate Adjectives in a Series*

Pairings testing provides the means to identify and appropriately punctuate the adjectives in a series whether they are all coordinate, all noncoordinate, or a mixture of both.

Coordinate adjectives are independent elements that individually modify the same noun or noun cluster. When used in a series, coordinate adjectives are separated from each other by commas (e.g., quick, strong, agile player).

Noncoordinate adjectives are cumulatively dependent modifiers that are indivisible parts of a noun cluster. As such, they cannot be separated by commas. A noun cluster is the grammatical element created when a noun and one or more adjectives combine to form what is seen and understood as a single entity (e.g., good old country boy).

Two pairings tests are used to identify and separate coordinate adjectives from those that are noncoordinate.

TEST 1—Adjectives in a pairing are coordinate if *and* can be inserted between them without spoiling the natural flow or changing the sense of a sentence.

TEST 2—Adjectives in a pairing are coordinate if *their order can be reversed* without spoiling or changing the sense of a sentence.

To test a series of adjectives, begin by locating the noun they modify. Next, in reverse order and working from right to left, couple the first (closest) and second adjectives immediately before the noun into pairing #1 and apply tests 1 and 2. In succession, couple adjectives two and three into pairing #2 and test, three and four into pairing #3 and test, etc., until all the adjectives in the series have been examined.

Adjectives that pass both tests are coordinate. Adjectives that fail either test are noncoordinate.

Pairings test results will determine <u>if</u> and <u>where</u> commas are appropriate whether all the adjectives in a series turn out to be coordinate (51a), all noncoordinate (51b), or there is a mix of both (51c).

51a. Series Adjectives All Coordinate

Apply both pairings tests to series adjectives in the sample sentence. Adjectives in pairings #1 and #2 pass Test 1 in example A, and they also pass Test 2 in example B. They are coordinate. Punctuation follows test results: Place commas between <u>tall</u> and <u>slender</u> and between <u>slender</u> and <u>blond</u> (example C).

Sample Sentence: John is the tall slender blond boy in that class.

Examples

A. John is the (tall <u>and</u> slender[#2]) (slender a<u>nd</u> blond[#1]) boy in that class.
B. John is the (slender tall[#2]) (blond slender[#1]) boy in that class.
C. John is the tall, slender, blond boy in that class.

NOTE: In a series, the articles *a, an* and *the* are always noncoordinate adjectives and are never followed by a comma.

51b. *Series Adjectives All Noncoordinate*

Apply both pairings tests to series adjectives in the sample sentence. Adjectives in pairings #1 and #2 fail Test 1 in example A, and they fail Test 2 in example B. They are noncoordinate. Punctuation follows test results: Do not place commas between <u>good</u> and <u>old</u> or between <u>old</u> and <u>country</u> (example C).

Sample Sentence: John is the good old country boy in that class.

Examples

A. John is the (good <u>and</u> old[#2]) (old <u>and</u> country[#1]) boy in that class.
B. John is the (old good[#2]) (country old[#1]) boy in that class.
C. John is the good_old_country boy in that class.

51c. *Series Is a Mix of Coordinate and Noncoordinate Adjectives*

Apply both pairings tests to series adjectives in the sample. Adjectives in pairings #1, #2, and #3 fail

Test 1 in example A, and they also fail Test 2 in example B. They are noncoordinate. Adjectives in pairings #4 and #5 pass Test 1 in example A, and they also pass Test 2 in example B. They are coordinate. Punctuation follows test results: Do not place commas between <u>blond</u> and <u>good</u>, between <u>good</u> and <u>old</u>, or between <u>old</u> and <u>country</u>. Place commas between <u>tall</u> and <u>slender</u> and between <u>slender</u> and <u>blond</u> (example C).

Sample Sentence: John is the tall slender blond good old country boy in that class.

<u>Examples</u>

A. John is the (tall <u>and</u> slender[#5]) (slender <u>and</u> blond[#4]) (blond <u>and</u> good[#3]) (good <u>and</u> old[#2]) (old <u>and</u> country[#1]) boy in that class.

B. John is the (slender tall[#5]) (blond slender[#4]) (good blond[#3]) (old good[#2]) (country old[#1]) boy in that class.

C. John is the tall, slender, blond _good_old_country boy in that class.

52. *Series Adjectives Modifying a Pronoun*

The same principles and techniques that determine comma use when series adjectives modify a noun or noun cluster apply when they modify a pronoun (e.g., tall, slender one) or pronoun cluster (e.g., wild_blue yonder).

53. Restrictive and Nonrestrictive Appositives, Clauses, Phrases

Appositives, clauses and phrases are classified as restrictive or nonrestrictive according to their function in a sentence. Whether restrictive or nonrestrictive, these sentence elements normally follow the noun or pronoun they modify. Restrictive sentence elements are not set off by commas or other punctuation, but nonrestrictive elements are.

Recall that an *appositive* is a word or group of words that means the same thing as the noun or pronoun it modifies (example 1).

An *independent clause* has a subject and predicate, expresses a complete thought, and can stand alone grammatically (example 2).

A *dependent clause* has a subject and predicate but does not express a complete thought and cannot stand alone grammatically (example 3). *If* in the example below is a subordinating conjunction.

A *phrase* is a group of related words which does not have both a subject and a predicate. A phrase may function as an adjective (in the tall tree in example 4) or as an adverb (on the floor in example 5).

Examples

1. George, my neighbor, is a helpful person.
2. Jack loves his new car.
3. If Jack loves his new car.
4. The bird in the tall tree is a crow.
5. He walked on the floor.

53a. Restrictive Sentence Elements

Restrictive appositives (examples 1 and 2), dependent clauses (examples 3 and 4), and phrases (examples 5 and 6) limit the scope of their sentences. They do it by identifying which person (examples 4-6), place, or thing (examples 1-3) is being discussed. Restrictive sentence elements are not set off my commas or other punctuation.

Examples

1. John Doe's novel <u>The Jelly Bean Ride</u> may become an American classic.
2. The name <u>Powhatan</u> originated with native American tribes in Virginia.
3. Antique clock collectors look for clocks <u>that have all their original parts</u>.
4. The carpenter <u>who uses his grandfather's tools</u> is the most skilled worker on the job.
5. The musician <u>strumming the red mandolin</u> is the most popular member of that band.
6. The fisherman <u>in the high rubber boots</u> is my father.

53b. Appositives and the Articles A, An, The

Appositives that follow a noun introduced by the indefinite articles *a* or *an* are usually considered nonrestrictive and set off by comma (example 1). Appositives that follow a noun introduced by the definite article *the* are usually considered restrictive and not set off by comma (example 2).

Examples

1. *An* old adage, "A penny saved is a penny earned," appeals to almost everyone.
2. *The* old adage_"A penny saved is a penny earned_" appeals to almost everyone.

53c. Nonrestrictive Sentence Elements

Nonrestrictive appositives, dependent clauses, and phrases merely provide additional information about a person, place or thing that has already been identified. These sentence elements are often found after a proper noun, which by definition is self-identifying. They may also follow a regular noun or pronoun that has already been identified by preceding modifiers.

53d. After Proper Nouns

When it is the subject, a proper noun automatically restricts the sentence because it is what is being discussed. Consequently, any information provided by a following appositive (examples 1 and 2), dependent clause (examples 3 and 4), or phrase (examples 5 and 6) can only be nonrestrictive and is set off by punctuation, most often by comma. Occasionally, dashes or parentheses are used as alternatives to the comma.

Examples

1. John Jay, a former governor of New York, was America's first Chief Justice of the Supreme Court.

2. George Washington, <u>America's first president</u>, was born in Virginia.
3. Thomas Edison, <u>who was an amazing inventor</u>, received over 100 patents.
4. The Empire State Building, <u>which was the tallest building in the world in 1931</u>, is still impressive.
5. The Wright brothers, <u>from Ohio</u>, made the first powered airplane flight in 1903.
6. Howard Hughes, <u>in a much publicized life</u>, was an industrialist, aviator, and film maker.

53e. After Preceding Modifiers

Preceding modifiers can restrict the scope of a sentence by identifying which person, place, or thing is being discussed. When this occurs, appositives, dependent clauses, or phrases that follow the subject are nonrestrictive and set off by punctuation, usually commas. Depending on the emphasis desired, parentheses or dashes may be used instead of commas. Preceding modifiers that can restrict a sentence include several groups of adjectives:

<u>Demonstrative</u>- -this, that, these, those.

<u>Descriptive</u>- -beautiful, ugly, blue, hot, etc.

<u>Limiting</u>- -several, few, four, many, tan, etc.

<u>Proper</u>- -French, Greek, Catholic, etc.

<u>Possessive</u>- -my, our, your, his, her, its, their.

In the sentences below, appositives follow a preceding possessive modifier (example 1) and a proper one (example 2).

Dependent clauses follow a demonstrative modifier (example 3) and a limiting one (example 4).

Phrases follow a proper modifier (example 5) and descriptive ones (example 6).

Examples

1. <u>My</u> cat, a wonderful little friend, came from the SPCA.
2. The <u>French</u> painting, a realistic copy of a Renoir, cost only $500.
3. <u>That</u> girl, who is strikingly attractive, has entered the contest.
4. <u>Sixteen</u> men, which is an entire shift, died in the mine accident.
5. <u>Virginia</u> drivers, in winter or summer, tend to be very polite.
6. <u>Tall, vibrant, maple</u> trees, displaying every color in the rainbow, are spectacular every fall.

53f. *Preceding Appositive Phrase*

A preceding appositive phrase is set off by comma (example).

Example

1. <u>A World War II relic</u>, the huge battleship sailed majestically into Norfolk's harbor bound for retirement and a storied place in naval history.

54. **We** *or* **Us** *Before a One-Word Appositive*

Do not place a comma between the subjective case pronoun *we* and a single-noun appositive that follows it (example 1).

Do not place a comma between the objective case pronoun *us* and a single-noun appositive that follows it (examples 2-4).

Examples

1. We students took our tests yesterday.
   (We is the subject of the sentence. Students is the appositive.)
2. Some of us students took our tests yesterday.
   (Us is the object of the preposition *of*. Students is the appositive.)
3. He gave the test to us students yesterday.
   (Us is the object of the preposition *to*. Students is the appositive.)
4. He gave us students the test yesterday.
   (Us is the object of the unstated but understood preposition *to*. Students is the appositive.)

55. *Relative Pronouns* **That** *and* **Which**

Clauses introduced by *that* are always restrictive. *Which*, on the other hand, may introduce clauses that are restrictive or clauses that are non-restrictive. However, generally using *which* only when it introduces a non-restrictive clause does provide a measure of grammatical consistency.

Note also how using *that* (example 1) or *which* (example 2) can alter the meaning of what is otherwise the same sentence. The first example implies there is more than one red vehicle; the second indicates there is only one.

Examples

1. The red vehicle *that* looks like a race car belongs to John Doe.
2. The red vehicle, *which* looks like a race car, belongs to John Doe.

OTHER THINGS ENGLISH

56. A, An, *before Consonant and Vowel Sounding Words*

Use the article a before consonant sounds, before words beginning with h when the h is pronounced, and before words beginning with the vowel u when it has the sound yoo (e.g., *a* book, *a* history, *a* unicorn).

Use the article an before a, e, i and o vowel sounds. (e.g., *an* apple, *an* eel, *an* island, *an* orange.)

Use an before words beginning with h when the h is not pronounced and before words beginning with the vowel u when is has the sound ugh (e.g. an honor, an umbrella).

57. *A.M., P.M.*

Ante meridiem (Latin for "before noon") describes the time between midnight (12 a.m.) and the following noon (12 p.m.). It is abbreviated with either capital or lowercase letters and can be presented with or without a colon (e.g., 6 A.M., 6 a.m.; 6:00 A.M., 6:00 a.m.).

Post meridiem (Latin for "after noon") describes the time between noon and midnight. It is abbreviated with either capital or lowercase letters (e.g., 6 P.M., 6 p.m.; 6:00 P.M., 6:00 p.m.).

58. *Apostrophe*

The apostrophe (') is used in forming contractions, to show possession (see "Forming Possessives"), and as an option in the formation of certain plurals.

58a. *With Contractions*

With contractions, an apostrophe is placed where there is the omission of numbers (e.g., '41 for 19̲4̲1), the omission of a letter (e.g., it's for it i̲s̲), of letters (e.g., they'll for they wi̲l̲l̲), or a combination of letters(s) and word(s) (e.g., o'clock for o̲f̲ t̲h̲e̲ clock).

58b. *With Plurals*

The apostrophe plus s̲ ('s) is necessary to form the plural ending of an abbreviation with periods (e.g., the plural of M.A. is M.A.'s). It is an option in forming the plural of abbreviations without periods, acronyms, and for decades (e.g., PAC's or PACs; VIP's or VIPs; 1920's or 1920s).

Letters referred to as letters, numbers as numbers, symbols as symbols, and words referred to as words are underlined or italicized. However, the '̲s̲ or s̲ ending that makes them plural is neither underlined nor italicized (e.g., *Q*'s or *Q*s; 7̲'s or 7s; t̲'s or *t*s; b̲e̲c̲a̲u̲s̲e̲'s or *becauses*).

In some plural constructions, the apostrophe is not optional but necessary in order to avoid confusion (e.g., there were six *a*'s, not six *a*s; six *i*'s, not six *i*s, etc.).

59. *Capitalization*

A proper noun names a specific person, place or thing (e.g., John Doe, Richmond, Easter). A proper noun is always capitalized.

59a. Common Nouns

A common noun names one or more members of a general class of persons, places or things (e.g., doctor, street, holiday). A common noun (examples 1, 2, 3) is not capitalized- -unless it is part of a proper name (examples 4, 5, 6).

<u>Examples</u>

1. The <u>navy</u> of the United States is a vital part of its defense.
2. He is taking <u>history</u> during the first semester.
3. The city <u>council</u> in Richmond voted on that last week.
4. The United States <u>N</u>avy has sent several ships there.
5. He is taking <u>H</u>istory 101 during the first semester.
6. The Richmond City <u>C</u>ouncil voted on that last week.

59b. Stand-Alone Personal Title

Capitalize a stand-alone personal title only when it is used as a substitute for the name of a particular person (example 1). Otherwise, stand-alone titles are generally lowercase (example 2).

Examples

1. Governor John Doe just called. In our conversation, the G̲overnor asked that all senior staff members meet here tonight.
2. The governor in every state will send a representative.

59c. *With Family Relationships*

Capitalize the name of a family relationship used in place of a proper name or in combination with a proper name when it is not preceded by an article (a, an, the) or by a possessive noun or pronoun (example 1). When it is preceded by a possessive pronoun (my, your, his, her, its, our, their) an article, or by a possessive noun, the name of a family relationship is lowercased (examples 2, 3, 4).

Examples

1. The other day G̲randfather and A̲unt Helen met with C̲ousin Lou at the restaurant.
2. The other day *my* grandfather and *his* a̲unt Helen met with *our* c̲ousin Lou at the restaurant.
3. Seated at the table were *a* grandfather, *an* a̲unt, and *the* c̲ousin Lou who lives in California.
4. *Bill's* c̲ousin Lou attended the meeting.

59d. *With Religion*

Capitalize (but do not underline or enclose in quotation marks) the names of religious books (New Testament, Bible, Koran, Old Testament, etc.), sacred writings (Talmud, Torah, Apocrypha,

Sunna, etc.), and divisions of the Bible (Genesis, Psalms, Matthew, Revelations, etc.).

Except when it refers to a pagan diety (the god Zeus; the gods Neptune, Proteus, etc.), capitalize the word God, noun references to God (Almighty, Allah, Holy Ghost, Holy Spirit, Jesus, Jehovah, Lord, Son of God, etc.), and pronouns that refer to God- -e.g., "And on the seventh day God ended His work which He had made."

59e. With Geographical Areas and Directions

Capitalize North, South, East, West, Southwest, etc., when they refer to a specific area or region (example 1) but lowercase them when referring to directions (example 2).

Examples

1. George lives in the South.
2. George lives south of the old town square.

59f. Days, Months, Holidays, Seasons

Capitalize the days of the week (Sunday, Saturday), months of the year (January, December), and holidays (Christmas, Easter); but do not capitalize the seasons (fall, winter, spring, summer, autumn)

59g. Titles

Capitalize the first, last, and all other important words in the titles of articles, books, essays, plays, poems, reports, short stories, and songs.

Do not capitalize the articles (a, an, the), the infinitive to, short conjunctions (and, but, or, if, as, etc.), or short prepositions (by, of, to, an, for, etc.)- - except when they are the first or last word in a title or were capitalized when the title was originally published.

Examples

1. "The Courtship of the Bee and the Moth"
(short story)
2. "How to Beat the System"
(article)
3. *They Are Rich but Needy*
(book)
4. *To the Victor Goes the Spoils*
(book)
5. "What a Fix She's In!"
(article)

59h. **AD** *and* **BC** *or* **CE** *and* **BCE**

Capitalize the period designations AD and BC or CE and BCE.

AD (anno Domini: "in the year of the Lord") is placed before numerals (e.g., AD 476). BC ("before Christ") is placed after numerals (e.g., 476 BC).

CE ("common era") and BCE ("before common era") are both placed after numerals (e.g., 476 CE; 476 BCE).

The designations, which may be used with or without periods, are equivalent but not interchangeable. In the same work, use either AD (A.D.) and BC (B.C.) or CE (C.E.) and BCE (B.C.E.)

59i. *Hyphenated Words in Titles*

In a title, always capitalize the first part of a hyphenated word (examples 1-5)

Capitalize any word in the second part that is a noun (example 2), a proper adjective (example 3), or that is equal to the first part in importance (example 5).

Examples

1. "Travelling on Route I-66."
   (Article)
2. "Pre-War Is an Anxious Time for Any Nation."
   (Article)
3. *The Rise of Anti-British Sentiment*
   (Book)
4. *The Clown with More Make-up than Face.*
   (Book)
5. "The Up-and-Coming Citizen"
   (Article)

60. *Collective Nouns and Verbs*

A collective noun is singular in form but represents or identifies a group, class, or category of persons, places, or things (e.g., family, team, jury, etc.).

When a group acts or exists as an undivided unit, its collective noun takes a singular verb (examples 1,3).

When a group acts or exists as a divided unit of individuals, its collective noun takes a plural verb (examples 2, 4).

Examples

1. The cast <u>has</u> "Break a leg" as its motto.
2. The cast <u>have</u> gone to their permanent homes for the holidays.
3. The jury <u>has</u> reached a verdict.
4. The jury <u>have</u> not been able to agree on a verdict.

60a. Number: Singluar or Plural?

When the noun *number* is preceded by the indefinite article <u>a</u>, it takes a plural verb (example 1). When it is preceded by the definite article <u>the</u>, it takes a singular verb (example 2).

Examples

1. <u>A</u> number of residents in that area <u>are</u> still to be counted.
2. <u>The</u> number of residents in that area <u>is</u> still to be counted.

60b. Fractional Number

When a fractional number is followed by a singular object of the preposition *of*, it takes a singular verb (examples 1, 3). When it is followed by a preposition whose object is plural, a fractional number takes a plural verb (examples 2, 4).

Examples

1. Three-quarters of the stor<u>e</u> <u>is</u> empty.
2. Three-quarters of the store<u>s</u> <u>are</u> empty.
3. One-third of <u>it</u> <u>is</u> here.
4. One-third of <u>them</u> <u>are</u> here.

61. *Colon or Dash Introduces an Appositive, Explanation, or Series*

Place a colon or a dash (more emphatic) after an independent clause that introduces a concluding appositive (examples 1,2), explanation (examples 3,4), or series (examples 5,6)

NOTE: Except for proper nouns, concluding words or phrases are all lowercase. Use of a capital letter to begin a concluding independent clause is optional.

Examples

1. They only care about one thing: money.
2. They only care about one thing- -money.
3. Whales are not fish: they are air-breathing mammals.
4. Whales are not fish- -they are air-breathing animals.
5. The very rich can afford very expensive toys: exotic cars, large yachts, and private jets.
6. The very rich can afford very expensive toys- - exotic cars, large yachts, and private jets.

62. *Colon with a Verb or Preposition That Introduces a Series*

As a general rule, a colon should not be used with a verb or preposition that introduces a series (examples 1,2).

However, there is an exception: A colon is placed after a verb or preposition that concludes a complete sentence before it introduces a series (examples 3,4).

Examples

1. The colors in that paint set are_red, white, blue, orange, yellow, and green.
2. The puzzle is composed of_squares, circles, and triangles.
3. In that train set, the principal parts are included_: engine, cars, track, and transformer. (*In that train set, the principal parts are included* is a complete sentence.)
4. They had serious problems to deal with_: old age, declining health, and a shrinking bank account. (*They had serious problems to deal with* is a complete sentence.)

63. *Dash with Preceding Word or Series*

Use a dash to set off an independent clause that sums up or explains a preceding word (example 1) or preceding series (example 2).

Examples

1. Money- -that is all they care about.
2. Exotic cars, large yachts, and private jets- -these are toys for the very rich.

64. *Forming Plurals*

Most singular nouns are made plural by adding an s (e.g., brick becomes bricks; bird, birds; car, cars, etc.)

Singular nouns ending in ch, s, sh, x and z are made plural by adding an es (e.g., church becomes churches; Jones, Joneses; bush, bushes; fox, foxes; fizz, fizzes, etc.)

Some irregular nouns are made plural by adding an _en_, others by a change in spelling (e.g., ox, oxen; child, children; man, men; woman, women; foot, feet; mouse, mice, etc.)

Nouns ending in _ful_ are made plural by adding an _s_ (e.g., spoonful becomes spoonfuls; handful, handfuls; teaspoonful, teaspoonfuls, etc.)

A few nouns have the same spelling for both singular and plural forms (e.g., deer, deer; Japanese, Japanese; sheep, sheep, etc.).

64a. *Compound Word That Includes a Noun*

When a compound word, hyphenated or unhyphenated, includes a noun and one or more modifiers (adjective, prepositional phrase, etc.), add the appropriate _s_ or _es_ to the _noun_ to make it plural.

For example, counselor-at-law becomes counselors-at-law; mother-in-law, mothers-in-law; hanger-on, hangers-on; commander in chief, commanders in chief; passer-by, passers-by; attorney general, attorneys general, etc.

A few compound words and certain contractions are exceptions to the standard rules for plurals. For example, Jack-o'-lantern (Jack-of-the-lantern) becomes Jack-o'-lanterns in the plural. The dictionary is the final arbiter.

64b. *Compound Word with Nouns of Equal Value*

When the nouns in a compound word are of equal value, add the appropriate _s_ or _es_ to the *last noun* in the compound to make it plural. For example, player-coach becomes player-coach<u>es</u>; actor-director, actor-director<u>s</u>; owner-driver, owner-driver<u>s</u>, etc.

64c. *Compound Word with No Noun*

When a compound word has no noun, add the appropriate <u>s</u> or <u>es</u> to the last word in the compound to make it plural. For example, forget-me-not becomes forget-me-not<u>s</u>; go-between, go-between<u>s</u>; take-off, take-off<u>s</u>, etc.

65. *Forming Possessives*

To form the possessive of singular nouns, including those ending in <u>s</u>, add an apostrophe plus an <u>s</u> ('s). For example, the possessive of Mrs. Jones is Mrs. Jones<u>'s</u>; Bob becomes Bob<u>'s</u>; teacher, teacher<u>'s</u>, etc.

65a. *Plural Noun*

To form the possessive of plural nouns ending in <u>s</u>, add only an apostrophe. For example, the possessive of Joneses is Joneses<u>'</u>; babies, babies<u>'</u>; doctors, doctors<u>'</u>, etc.

To form the possessive of plural nouns not ending in <u>s</u>, add an apostrophe plus an <u>s</u> ('s). For example, the possessive of children is children<u>'s</u>; men, men<u>'s</u>; women, women<u>'s</u>, etc.

65b. *Individual Possession or Ownership*

To indicate individual possession or ownership, add an apostrophe plus <u>s</u> ('s) to each separate owner.

Example

Tom's and George's horses won races last year. (Tom had horses that won races, and George had horses that won races.)

65c. *Joint Possession or Ownership*

To indicate joint possession or ownership, add an apostrophe plus s ('s) only to the last owner in a pairing (example 1) or to the last owner in a series of owners (example 2).

Examples

1. Tom and George's horses won races last year. (Horses owned jointly by Tom and George won races.)
2. Tom, George, James and John's horses won races last year. (Horses owned jointly by Tom, George, James, and John won races.)

65d. *Animate Objects*

An apostrophe may be used with animate objects or with organizations made up of people as a more direct way of expressing possession or connection where an of phrase could be used to convey the same meaning. For example, doctor's responsibility has the same meaning as responsibility of the doctor; generals' decision means the same as decision of the generals; fire department's budget, budget of the fire department, etc.

65e. *Inanimate Objects*

With inanimate objects, except for expressions of time and measurement (e.g., six week's salary, a morning's promise, a dime's worth, a stone's throw, etc.) possession is shown by combining the preposition of with a noun. The apostrophe is not used. For example, it is the heel of a boot- -not the boot's heel; the face of the cliff- -not the cliff's face; the façade of a building- -not the building's facade, etc.

65f. *Compound Word*

To form the possessive of a singular compound word, hyphenated or unhyphenated, add an apostrophe plus s ('s) to the last word in the compound. For example, counselor-at-law becomes counselor-at-law's; attorney general, attorney general's; owner-driver, owner-driver's; passer-by, passer-by's; go-between, go-between's, commander in chief, commander in chief's, etc.

To form the possessive of a plural compound word not ending in s, add an apostrophe plus s ('s) to the last word in the compound. For example, counselors-at-law becomes counselors-at-law's, attorneys general, attorneys general's; passers-by, passers-by's, commanders in chief, commanders in chief's, etc.

To form the possessive of a plural compound word ending in s, place only an apostrophe after the s. For example, forget-me-nots becomes forget-me-nots'; owner-drivers, owner-drivers'; go-betweens, go-betweens', etc.

65g. Indefinite Pronoun

To form the possessive of an indefinite pronoun, add an apostrophe plus s ('s). For example, everybody becomes everybody's; anyone, anyone's; something, something's, etc.

65h. Personal Pronoun

Unlike indefinite pronouns and nouns, *personal pronouns **never** include an apostrophe.* Personal pronouns must change form to show possession. For example, the pronoun I becomes my or mine in its possessive form; we changes to our or ours; you to your or yours; he to his; she to her or hers; it to its; they to their or theirs; who to whose.

65i. Pronouns Ending in **Self** *or* **Selves**

Do not use an apostrophe with pronouns ending in self or selves.

Examples

1. One should try to help oneself (not one'self, ones'elf, etc.)
2. They owned the horses themselves (not themselve's, themselves', etc.)

66. Hyphen

66a. Hyphens to Form Compound Adjectives

Place a hyphen between words used together to form a single compound adjective that precedes a noun (example 1). However, when the same modifying words come after the noun, the hyphen is omitted (example 2).

Examples

1. The candidate made several off-the-record comments.
2. The candidate made several comment off_the_record.

66b. Hyphens Omitted between -ly, -er, or -est Ending Modifiers

The hyphen is omitted between preceding modifiers if one of them is an adverb ending in -ly (example 1), a comparative (-er ending) adjective (example 2), or a superlative (-est ending) adjective (example 3).

Examples

1. The candidate made several blatantly_false comments.
2. The candidate is among the better_educated politicians in this state.
3. The candidate is the best_educated politician in this state.

66c. Compound Adjectives with the Same Base Word

Two or more compound adjectives that have the same base word (e.g., year, below) and modify the same noun (e.g., players, below) always retain their hyphens (examples 1,2). However, their base word may be used with only the final compound modifier (example 2).

Examples

1. Those first-<u>year</u>, second-<u>year</u>, and third-<u>year</u> players are the best.
2. Those first-, second-, and third-<u>year</u> players are the best.

66d. Compound Numbers, Fractions

Use a hyphen in fractions (e.g., three-fifths) and in compound numbers from twenty-one to ninety-nine when they are written out. Use the slash (/) for numerical fractions (e.g., 3/5, 1 3/5 miles, etc.

66e. Hyphenated Measurements

Measurements that come before the noun they modify are hyphenated and written in the singular (examples 1, 2, 5, 7, 9, 11).

Each unit of measure that follows the noun it refers to is written in the plural and without internal hyphens or commas (e.g., the *length* in example 6; *height, weight,* 8; *time,* 10; *deadline,* 12, 13).

If the symbols <u>'</u> or <u>"</u> are used in place of the words foot (feet) or inch(es), either <u>by</u> (example 3) or <u>x</u> (example 4) is used between individual measurements. When symbols are used, the format is the same whether the measurements come before or after the noun they modify (examples 3, 4).

Examples

1. They had a 10-foot-by-17-foot-6-inch rug.
2. They had a ten-foot-by-seventeen-foot-six-inch rug.

3. They had a 10' by 17'6" rug. (The rug they had is 10' by 17'6".)
4. They had a 10' x 17'6" rug. (The rug they had is 10' x 17'6".)
5. His prize antique was a 125-foot, three-masted schooner.
6. His prize antique schooner was 125 feet long and three masted.
7. Jim is a 6-foot-3-inch, 225-pound-11-ounce man.
8. Jim is 6 feet 3 inches tall and weighs 225 pounds 11 ounces.
9. John's 2-hour-40-minute-13-second time is his best in the annual spring race.
10. John's best time in the annual spring race is 2 hours 40 minutes 13 seconds.
11. The 3-year-6-month-15-day deadline was established last year.
12. The deadline established late last year was 3 years 6 months 15 days.
    OR
13. The deadline established late last year was three years six months fifteen days.

66f. Measurement as Part of a Noun

A measurement that is part of a noun is always hyphenated (example 1, 2).

Examples

1. The 7-footer in the blue jersey is John Doe.
2. He ordered another six-pack of soda.

66g. Numbers with Ages

With numbers spelled out or as Arabic numerals, use hyphens with ages to form a preceding modifier (examples 1, 2). No hyphens are used when the modifying compound follows the noun (examples 3, 4). Use hyphens with ages to form a compound that is a noun (examples 5, 6).

Examples

1. There is a three-year-old horse.
2. There is a 3-year-old horse.
3. That horse is three years old.
4. That horse is 3 years old.
5. That is one fast three-year-old.
6. That is one fast 3-year-old.

66h. Age *and* Aged

Use the noun age (example 1) and the adjective aged (example 2).

Examples

1. Jim's age is 36 on our records.
2. Jim Smith, aged 36, has just retired with a disability.

66i. Same Spelling But Different Words

Use the hyphen to differentiate between words that have the same spelling but a different meaning, such as re-tire (to put tires on again) and retire (to withdraw); re-cover (to cover again) and recover (to regain); and <u>re-creation </u>(to create again) and <u>recreation </u>(refreshment in mind or body by some form of play or relaxation), etc.

67. *Latin Abbreviations*

A comma should be used after certain Latin abbreviations and their translations such as <u>i.e</u>. (that is, namely) and <u>e.g.</u> (for example). Depending on the emphasis desired, preceding punctuation may be a comma (examples 1, 1a, 6, 6a), opening parenthesis (examples 2, 2a, 7, 7a), or a dash (examples 3, 3a, 8, 8a). The preceding punctuation may be a semicolon if the abbreviation or its translation begins the second independent clause in a compound sentence (examples 4, 5, 9, 10).

67a. **I.E.** *(that is)*

<u>Examples</u>

1. Police have only one viable suspect, i.e., John Doe.
1a. Police have only one viable suspect, i.e., John Doe, for that crime.
2. Police have only one viable suspect (i.e., John Doe).
2a. Police have only one viable suspect (i.e., John Doe) for that crime.
3. Police have only one viable suspect- -i.e., John Doe.
3a. Police have only one viable suspect- -i.e., John Doe- -for that crime.

4. Police have only one viable suspect; i.e., John Doe was the only person at the crime scene.
5. Police have only one viable suspect; that is, John Doe was the only person at the crime scene.

67b. E.G. *(for example)*

Examples

6. Several scientific advances in medicine have also become important elements in law enforcement; e.g., DNA testing.
6a. Several scientific advances in medicine, for example, DNA testing, have also become important elements in law enforcement.
7. Several scientific advances in medicine have also become important elements in law enforcement (e.g., DNA testing).
7a. Several scientific advances in medicine (for example, DNA testing) have also become important elements in law enforcement.
8. Several scientific advances in medicine have also become important elements in law enforcement- -e.g., DNA testing.
8a. Several scientific advances in medicine- -for example, DNA testing- -have also become important elements in law enforcement.
9. Several scientific advances in medicine have also become important elements in law enforcement; e.g., DNA testing has led to a number of convictions.

10. Several scientific advances in medicine have also become important elements in law enforcement; for example, DNA testing has led to a number of convictions.

67c. Etc. *(and so forth, and others)*

The Latin abbreviation *etc.* or its translation (and so forth, and others) should be set off with commas (examples 1,2) unless it concludes a sentence (examples 3,4).

Examples
1. They wanted the bats, balls, masks, uniforms, etc., to be stored at school.
2. They wanted the bats, balls, masks, uniforms, and so forth, to be stored at school.
3. The school storage room contained the bat, balls, masks, uniforms, etc.
4. The school storage room contained the bats, balls, masks, uniforms, and so forth.

68. *Linking Verbs*

Linking verbs express a condition- -not an action. A linking verb joins or links the subject of a sentence with a predicate noun, predicate adjective, or -predicate pronoun. Linking verbs include all the variations of the verb to be* (am, are, be, been, being, is, was, were), verbs of the five senses- -see, hear, touch, taste, smell, and other verbs that express condition such as appear, became, become, feel, grow look, remain, sound, etc. It is the number (singular or plural) of the subject- -not a predicate noun or pronoun- -that determines the number of the linking verb.

Examples

1. The heart of the team is the defensive players.
   (The subject [heart] is singular, so the linking verb [is] must also be singular.)
2. The defensive players are the heart of the team.
   (The subject [players] is plural, so the linking verb [are] must also be plural.)

* To be is interchangeable with be as the collective term for the same irregular linking verb and its many forms.

68a. Predicate Noun

A predicate noun is a noun that follows a linking verb, completes the predicate, and stands for or contrasts with the person, place, or thing that is the subject of a sentence.

Examples

1. George is the president of the company.
   (President stands for the subject George.)
2. Whales are not fish.
   (Fish contrasts with the subject whales, which are air-breathing mammals.)

68b. Predicate Adjective

A predicate adjective is an adjective that follows a linking verb, completes the predicate, and limits or describes the person, place or thing that is the subject of the sentence.

Examples

1. Julie became 15 years old on Saturday.
   (The predicate adjective <u>15 years old</u> limits the age of the subject.)
2. George feels bad on cold days like this.
   (The predicate adjective <u>bad </u>describes the subject's [George's] physical, mental, or emotional condition.)

NOTE: Don't confuse <u>bad</u>, an adjective which can only modify a noun or pronoun, with the adverb <u>badly</u>. Adverbs can only modify verbs, adjectives, or other adverbs. Had the sentence above been written this way: George feels <u>badly</u>..., <u>badly</u> would modify *feels* and describe George's ability to sense what he physically touches.

68c. *Predicate Pronoun*

A predicate pronoun is a pronoun that follows a linking verb, completes the predicate, and stands for or contrasts with the person, place or thing that is the subject of the sentence. Predicate pronouns are always in the subjective case and include the personal pronouns I, we, you*, he, she, it, they; and the relative/interrogative pronouns who and whoever**.

Examples

1. That is (<u>he</u>, him) at the bottom of the stairs.
   (Since it follows the linking verb <u>is</u>, the personal pronoun must be the subjective case <u>he</u>.)
2. The winner of the contest was (<u>who</u>, whom)?
   (Since it follows the linking verb <u>was</u>, the

relative/interrogative pronoun must be the subjective case <u>who</u>.)

*The form and spelling of the second person pronoun <u>you</u> is the same whether it is singular or plural or whether its sentence function places it in the subjective or objective case. <u>You</u> always takes a plural verb.

**<u>Whom</u> and <u>whomever</u> are the objective case forms for the relative/interrogative pronoun <u>who</u>. Personal pronouns in the objective case are me, us, you, him, her, it, or them.

69. *Literary Present Tense*

Use the literary present tense (example 1) when discussing the work of an author, even one who is deceased, and when describing action or presenting dialogue from the work (example 2).

<u>Examples</u>

1. The late John Doe masterfully opens the final scene with Penelope looking out of the window.
2. "I must leave right now," she says, and her eyes fill with tears.

70. *Parentheses, Dashes, or Commas with Regular Material*

Regular material (copy not in quotations) can be set off from other text using parentheses, dashes, or commas. Parentheses provide the least emphasis, dashes the most, and commas are used to present material whose importance lies somewhere in between.

70a. *Regular Sentence Inserted Using Parentheses*

Parentheses ( ) are always used in pairs, one before and one after the material they enclose. A comma is never placed before an opening parenthesis, but it may be used after a closing parenthesis.

The inserted sentence is preceded by an opening parenthesis and begins with a lowercase letter unless its own first word is a proper noun. It concludes with a closing parenthesis.

If a sentence that originally ended with a period is inserted somewhere in the middle of another sentence using parentheses, the period is deleted (example 1). If it originally ended with a question mark (example 2), or an exclamation point (example 3), that punctuation is retained and followed by a closing parenthesis. If the insertion concludes a sentence, the appropriate end punctuation (e.g., period, question mark, or exclamation point) is placed after the concluding parenthesis (example 4).

Examples

1. The bride's father was so happy (the bride and groom are a picture-perfect couple_) that he even danced with his new in-laws.
2. The bride's father was so happy (aren't the bride and groom a picture-perfect couple?) that he even danced with his new in-laws.
3. The bride's father was so happy (his daughter and new son-in-law look like movie stars!) that he even danced with his new in-laws.
4. The bride's father was so happy (his daughter and new son-in-law look like movie stars!).

70b. Regular Fragment inside Parentheses

A fragment inserted into another sentence using parentheses is all lowercase unless it contains proper nouns. If the fragment was originally followed by a period, the period is deleted (example 1). If it originally ended with a question mark (example 2) or an exclamation point (example 3), that punctuation is retained and followed by a closing parenthesis. If the insertion concludes a sentence, the appropriate end punctuation is placed after its closing parenthesis (example 4).

Examples

1. The bride's father (a relatively young man) pretended that he was happy.
2. The bride's father (a cousin of yours?) pretended that he was happy.
3. The bride's father (a crafty old fox!) pretended that he was happy.
4. The bride's father reminded me of a sly forest creature (a crafty old fox!).

70c. Freestanding Parentheses

A regular sentence within freestanding parentheses begins with a capital letter. It concludes with its original end punctuation- -period, question mark, or exclamation point. No punctuation is placed outside freestanding parentheses.

Example

1. The bride's father was very happy. (The bride and groom are a picture-perfect couple.)

70d. *Regular Sentence Inserted Using Dashes*

The dash (- -) is typed as two hyphens with no space between it and the text that precedes or follows it.

The inserted sentence is preceded by a dash and begins with a lowercase letter unless its own first word is a proper noun. It concludes with a dash.

If a sentence that originally ended with a period is inserted somewhere in the middle of another sentence, the opening and closing dashes are retained, but the period is deleted (example 1). If it originally ended with a question mark (example 2) or an exclamation point (example 3), that punctuation is retained and followed by a dash. If it concludes a sentence (example 4), the insertion's closing dash is replaced by the appropriate end punctuation (e.g., period, question mark, or exclamation point.)

Examples

1. The bride's father was so happy- -the bride and groom are a picture-perfect couple_- -that he even danced with his new in-laws.
2. The bride's father was so happy- -aren't the bride and groom a picture-perfect couple?- -that he even danced with his new in-laws.
3. The bride's father was so happy- -his new son-in-law just won the lottery!- -that he even danced with his new in-laws.
4. The bride's father was so happy- -his new son-in-law just won the lottery!

70e. Regular Fragment inside Dashes

A fragment inserted into another sentence using dashes is all lowercase unless it contains proper nouns. If the fragment was originally followed by a period, it is placed within dashes, but the period is deleted (example 1). If it originally ended with a question mark (example 2) or an exclamation point (example 3), that punctuation is retained and followed by a dash. If it concludes a sentence (example 4), the insertion's closing dash is replaced by the appropriate end punctuation.

<u>Examples</u>

1. The bride's father- -a relatively young man_- -pretended that he was happy.
2. The bride's father- -a cousin of yours<u>?</u>- -pretended that he was happy.
3. The bride's father- -a crafty old fox<u>!</u>- -pretended that he was happy.
4. The bride's father reminded me of a sly forest creature- -a crafty old fox<u>!</u>

70f. Regular Sentence Inserted Using Commas

The inserted sentence is preceded by a comma and begins with a lowercase letter unless its own first word is a proper noun. If a sentence that originally ended with a period is inserted somewhere in the middle of another sentence, it is preceded by a comma, and its period is replaced by a comma (example 1). If it originally ended with a question mark (example 2) or an exclamation point (example 3), that punctuation is retained.

Examples

1. The bride's father was so happy, the bride and groom are a picture-perfect couple, that he even danced with his new in-laws.
2. The bride's father was so happy, aren't the bride and groom a picture-perfect couple? that he even danced with his new in-laws.
3. The bride's father was so happy, his daughter and new son-in-law look like movie stars! that he even danced with his new in-laws.

70g. Regular Fragment inside Commas

A fragment inserted into another sentence using commas is all lowercase unless it contains proper nouns. If a fragment was originally followed by a period, it is placed within commas, and the period is deleted (example 1). If it originally ended with a question mark (example 2) or an exclamation point (example 3), that punctuation is retained. If it concludes a sentence (example 4), the insertion is followed by the appropriate end punctuation.

Examples

1. The bride's father, a relatively young man, pretended that he was happy.
2. The bride's father, a cousin of yours? pretended that he was happy.
3. The bride's father, a crafty old fox! pretended that he was happy.
4. The bride's father reminded me of a sly forest creature, a crafty old fox!

71. Indefinite Pronouns

The indefinite pronoun is less exact than other pronouns and references a person, place, or thing in a general, nonspecific manner.

Indefinite pronouns are always third person. The vast majority are singular and always take a singular verb, even when followed by a prepositional phrase with a plural object (examples 1-4). Among the most frequently used are another, each, either, much, neither, one and any compound of body (e.g., anybody, everybody, nobody, somebody), one (e.g. anyone, everyone, no one, someone), or thing (e.g., anything, everything, nothing, something).

An indefinite pronoun (example 5) may also function as a regular adjective (example 6) or as a possessive adjective (examples 7, 8) modifying a singular noun.

Examples

1. *Each* of the new students is ready for the test.
2. *Everybody* in the three morning classes is in the pool.
3. *Everyone* or (*every one*) of the contestants is wearing red, white and blue.
4. *Everything* in all of those stores is now on sale.
5. *Neither* has arrived on time.
6. *Neither* student has arrived on time.
7. *Neither's* student has arrived on time.
8. *Everybody's* car is in the student parking lot.

71a. Exception I (*Indefinite Pronouns That Are Always Plural*)

A handful of indefinite pronouns (e.g., both, few, many, several) are plural and always take a plural verb (examples 1,2). They may also be used as adjectives modifying plural nouns (example 3).

Examples

1. *Many* of the cups <u>are</u> on the table.
2. *Many* <u>are</u> on the table.
3. *Many* cups <u>are</u> on the table.

71b. Exception II (*Indefinite Pronouns That Can Be Singular or Plural*)

A few indefinite pronouns (e.g., all, any, more, most, some) can be singular or plural, depending on the object of the prepositional phrase that immediately follows them. The prepositional phrase may be stated (examples 1, 3, 5) or implied (examples 2, 4). In either case, when the preposition's object is singular, the verb will be singular (examples 3, 4). When the object is plural, the verb will be plural (examples 1, 2, 5). Each of these five pronouns may also be used as an adjective modifying a singular (example 6) or a plural (example 7) noun.

Examples

1. *Some* of the <u>uniforms</u> <u>are</u> in the laundry.
2. *Some* <u>are</u> in the laundry.
3. *Most* of the <u>sugar</u> <u>is</u> already on the shelf.
4. *Most* is already on the shelf.

5. *Most* of the sacks of sugar are already on the shelf.
6. *All* chocolate tastes good.
7. *All* contestants were given free passes.

71c. None: The Unique Indefinite Pronoun

The indefinite pronoun *none* is unique in its ability to convey a subtle but distinct difference in meaning. When *none* is to mean "not a single one," it takes a singular verb (example 1). When *none* refers to a group or collection, its verb is plural (example 2).

Examples

1. *None* of those tractors is strong enough to pull that load.
   (Not a single tractor is strong enough to pull the load.)
2. *None* of those tractors are strong enough to pull that load.
   (All of those tractors are too weak to pull the load.)

71d. Compound Subjects with **Each** *or* **Every**

Compound subjects with and that are preceded by *each* (examples 1, 2) or *every* (examples 3, 4) always take a singular verb.

Examples

1. *Each* stove and refrigerator has been reduced in price.
2. *Each* stove, refrigerator, and microwave oven has been reduced in price.

3. *Every* stove and refrigerator <u>is</u> on the truck.
4. *Every* stove, refrigerator and microwave oven <u>is</u> on the truck.

71e. *Compound Subjects with* **And**

Except for compound subjects preceded by *each* or *every* and word compounds treated as a single entity (e.g., bacon and eggs is…, etc.), singular and plural subjects joined by *and*, regardless of the order of the subjects, always take a plural verb (examples 1,2).

<u>Examples</u>

1. *He* and the *players* <u>are</u> making that decision.
2. The *players* and he <u>are</u> making that decision.

71f. *Compound Subjects With* **Or** *or* **Nor**

When compound subjects are joined by *or* or *nor*, their verb always agrees with the subject that follows *or* or *nor* (examples 1, 2). This is true even if a singular indefinite pronoun is positioned before the first subject (examples 3, 4)

<u>Examples</u>

1. The players or the *owner* <u>is</u> going to win the dispute.
2. The owner or the *players* <u>are</u> going to win the dispute.
3. Neither the *players* nor he <u>is</u> going to win the dispute.
4. Neither he nor the *players* <u>are</u> going to win the dispute.

71g. Pronoun Agreement with **Or** or **Nor**

When a compound subject joined by or or nor is an antecedent, the pronoun that refers back to it always agrees with the subject that follows or or nor. If one subject is singular and one is plural, avoid awkward sentence constructions (example 1) by placing the plural subject after or or nor (example 2).

Examples

1. Either the girls or Sue is going to get her way.
2. Either Sue or the girls are going to their way.

71h. One of, Only one of, The only one of

The phrases one of and only one of are always completed with a plural object of the preposition. When followed by a relative clause, the subject of the clause (who, which, or that) and its verb will both be plural (examples 1, 2).

The phrase the only one of is also completed with a plural object of the preposition. However, when the definite article *the* precedes a phrase containing the pronoun *one*, the verb in a following relative clause must be singular (example 3). In the first two examples, the antecedent of *who* is *pilots*. In example 3, the antecedent of *who* is *one*.

Examples

1. John Doe is one of the *pilots* who were there.
2. John Doe is only one of the *pilots* who were there.
3. John Doe is *the* only *one* of the pilots who was there.

71i. One, One's; He, His; She, Her

One and one's can refer back to the indefinite pronoun *one* (example 1). It is also correct for *he* or *his* (example 2), *she* or *her* (example 3), or *he* or *she* or *his* or *her* to refer back to *one* (example 4).

Examples

1. One likes to shop at a discount store when *one* can save *one's* money.
2. One likes to shop at a discount store when *he* can save *his* money.
3. One likes to shop at a discount store when *she* can save *her* money.
4. One likes to shop at a discount store when *he* or *she* can save *his* or *her* money.

71j. Each Other, One Another

There are only two reciprocal pronouns in the English language: *each other* and *one another*. Each other references the interaction of two persons or things (example 1). One another is used when the interaction involves three or more persons or things (example 2).

Examples

1. My father and I love *each other*.
2. My father, mother, brother, sister and I love *one another*.

71k. Pronouns after **As** or **Than**

The case of a pronoun (subjective or objective) used after *as* or *than* is the same whether a sentence is complete (examples 1, 3, 5), or portions of it are unstated but understood (examples 2, 4, 6).

Examples

1. John was just as thoughtful as she was.
2. John was just as thoughtful as she.
3. Sue can sing better than I can.
4. Sue can sing better than I.
5. The extra time helped John more than it helped me.
6. The extra time helped John more than me.

71l. *Intensive and Reflexive Pronouns*

Intensive and reflexive pronouns both end with either the singular *self* or the plural *selves*. An intensive pronoun adds emphasis to the word it follows (example1). A reflexive pronoun is the same person or thing that it refers back to as the subject of a sentence (example 2). Avoid the common mistake of using an intensive or reflexive pronoun in place of a personal pronoun (examples 3, 4).

Examples

1. I *myself* am to blame for that mistake.
2. He made that mistake *himself*.
3. They asked *me* (not "myself") to speak to the team.
4. The team asked to speak with Larry and *me* (not "myself") about that.

71m. Pronoun Order in a Compound

The order of personal pronouns used in a compound is second person, third person, first person (examples 1, 2).

Examples

1. *You, he* and *I* will decide on the cake.
2. They will depend on *you, him and me*.

71n. Relative Pronouns **That** *and* **Which**

Clauses introduced by *that* are always restrictive. *Which,* on the other hand, may introduce clauses that are restrictive or clauses that are non-restrictive. However, generally using *which* only when it introduces a non-restrictive clause does provide a measure of grammatical consistency.

Note also how using *that* (example 1) or *which* (example 2) can alter the meaning of what is otherwise the same sentence. The first example implies there is more than one red vehicle; the second indicates there is only one.

Examples

1. The red vehicle *that* looks like a race car belongs to John Doe.
2. The red vehicle, *which* looks like a race car, belongs to John Doe.

71o. Determining the Correct Pronoun to join with a Noun or another Pronoun

To determine whether a pronoun joined with a noun should be in the subjective case (example 1) or the objective (example 2), delete the noun and choose the form of the pronoun that sounds correct. The procedure is the same when selecting the correct case for each of two pronouns that are joined. In turn, delete each of the pronouns and choose the form for the remaining one that sounds correct (examples 3, 4).

Examples

1. Tom and <u>I</u> (not "me") took the bus to school. (Delete Tom. <u>I</u> took the bus to school, not <u>me</u> took the bus to school.)
2. The teacher showed Tom and <u>me</u> (not "I") the answer. (Delete Tom. The teacher showed <u>me</u>, not the teacher showed <u>I</u>.)
3. <u>He</u> and <u>I</u> (not "him" and I or he and "me") took the bus to school.
4. The teacher showed <u>you</u> and <u>me</u> (not you and "I") the answer.

71p. *Pronoun before a Gerund or Participle*

Use a possessive pronoun or noun before a gerund (examples 1,3). Use a regular pronoun or noun before a participle (examples 2,4). Recall, a gerund is an *-ing* or *-ed* ending verbal used as a noun. A participle is an *-ing* or *-ed* ending verbal functioning as an adjective.

Examples

1. The award recognized <u>his</u> standing in the community.
2. The witness recognized <u>him</u> standing in the lineup.

3. The <u>boat's</u> sinking in the harbor will be investigated.
4. The <u>boat</u> sinking in the harbor belongs to John Doe.

72. *Slash*

The slash (also solidus, virgule) is a slant line (/) used to signal options (examples 1 and 2) or to represent the word *per* (example 3).

<u>Examples</u>

1. Instructors use a pass/fail (i.e., pass *or* fail) grading system in that course.
2. Students can take science and/or math courses (i.e., students can take courses in science, in math, or in both).
3. The miles/gallon (i.e., miles *per* gallon) rating for that car is 19 in the city and 23 on the highway.

73. *Spacing with Punctuation*

Where there is an option, whichever the choice, its use should be consistent throughout the same work.

<u>Examples</u>

Five spaces
1. Paragraph indentation

Either one or two spaces
2. After sentence ending punctuation.
3. After sentence ending colon.

One space

4. After a colon in a title.
5. After a comma.
6. After exclamation point within a sentence.
7. Before and after hyphen used as a minus sign.
8. Before and after parentheses inside a sentence.
9. After periods following initials in a personal name.
10. After question mark within a sentence.
11. Before and after a slash between lines of poetry.
12. After a semicolon.

No Space

13. Before or after a colon in ratios.
14. Before or after a hyphen between words.
15. After the closing parenthesis at the end of a sentence.
16. Before periods in abbreviations.
17. Before or after a slash between words, etc.
18. Before the first word or after the last word within parentheses.

74. *Verb Tenses*

Tense is the time or time frame expressed by a verb.

A verb has four principal parts: present tense (also known variously as the "base," "dictionary," or "plain" form, etc.), past tense, past participle, and present participle.

Regular verbs form the past tense and past participle by adding d, ed, or t to the present tense (e.g., shove, shoved, shoved; talk, talked, talked; weep, wept, wept). The present participle is formed by adding <u>ing</u> to the present tense (e.g., shove, shoving; talk, talking; weep, weeping).

The dictionary provides the principal parts of irregular verbs (e.g., lie, lay, lain, lying, etc.).

74a. *Present Tense*

The present tense expresses action (example 1) or a state of being (example 2) in the present, a habitual action (example 3), or a universal truth (example 4). The past tense is used to express something once believed that is no longer considered valid (example 5).

<u>Examples</u>

1. He <u>sings</u> at the Doe Theatre.
2. I <u>am</u> at home.
3. He never <u>forgets</u> to bring a dictionary.
4. The sun <u>is</u> the center of our solar system.
5. Many ancient cultures <u>believed</u> that the earth <u>was</u> the center of our solar system.

74b. *Past Tense*

The past tense expresses an action completed in the past (example 1), two or more actions completed at approximately the same time in the past (example 2), or a state of being in the past (example 3). Except for the verb *be*, the past tense is formed by ending the second principal part of a verb with <u>d</u>, <u>ed</u>, or <u>t</u>, as appropriate.

Examples

1. She <u>managed</u> that business for ten years.
2. She <u>managed</u> that business and <u>generated</u> a profit for ten years.
3. He <u>was</u> at that meeting.

74c. *Future Tense*

The future tense expresses action that will occur in the future. It is formed by combining the auxiliary verbs *shall* or *will* with the present tense (examples 1-3).

Examples

1. I <u>shall sing</u> (or <u>will sing</u>) next week.
2. You <u>will sing</u> next week.
3. She <u>will sing</u> next week.

74d. *Perfect Tenses*

The perfect tenses are formed by combining the past participle with a form of the auxiliary verb *have*.

74e. *Present Perfect Tense*

The present perfect tense expresses an action begun in the past that is now completed (example 1), an action begun in the past and continuing into the present (example 2), or an habitual action completed at some non-specific time in the past (examples 3,4). The present perfect tense is formed by combining the auxiliary verbs *has* or *have* with the past participle.

Examples

1. He <u>has</u> <u>talked</u> about that possibility in the past.
2. He <u>has</u> <u>talked</u> about that possibility for years.
3. In the past, he <u>has</u> always <u>talked</u> about that possibility.
4. In the past, they <u>have</u> always <u>talked</u> about that possibility.

74f. *Past Perfect Tense*

The past perfect tense is used to indicate that one past action occurred before another past action. The past perfect tense is formed by combining the auxiliary verb *had* with the past participle.

Example

1. He <u>had</u> <u>paid</u> for the car before he found out that it was a lemon.

74g. *Future Perfect Tense*

The future perfect tense is used to indicate that one action will be completed before another action at some time in the future. The future perfect tense is formed by combining *shall have* (example 1) or *will have* (examples 2,3) with the past participle.

Examples

1. I <u>shall have</u> (or will have) <u>completed</u> that paper before we leave tomorrow.
2. You <u>will have completed</u> that paper by the time they get here.
3. They <u>will have completed</u> that paper before next week's deadline.

74h. Progressive Tenses

The progressive tenses express or emphasize action that is (example 1), was (example 2), or will be (example 3) on-going, continuing. Progressive tenses are formed by combining certain helping verbs with the present participle (*ing* form of a verb). Helping verbs used when forming the various progressive tenses include *am, are, be, been, can, could, had, has, have, may, might, must, shall, should, was, were, will, would*.

Examples

1. I am working on that right now.
2. We have been working on that for years.
3. I shall be working on that for the rest of the year.

74i. Emphatic Tenses

The emphatic tenses are used with questions (examples 1, 2) and for emphasis in positive (example 3) or negative (example 4) statements. The emphatic tenses are formed by combining the appropriate auxiliary verb, *do, does,* or *did*, with the present tense.

Examples

1. Did you talk to him yesterday?
2. Does he really believe that?
3. I do want to see that play.
4. I do not want to see that play.

75. *Underlining (Italics) Versus Quotation Marks for Names and Titles*

Originally, the underline was used in writing and typing to indicate which word or words were to appear in slanted type (italics) when a manuscript, poem, play, etc., was published. When two or more words are underlined, the line should be continuous and include the space between them. Computers have made the choice between underlining or italicizing a readily available option, although underlining is still preferred for most academic work. Whichever the choice, its use should be consistent throughout the same work.

As a general rule, underline or italicize the titles of <u>whole</u> entities such as newspapers, novels, and motion pictures (e.g., <u>The Doetown Post-Dispatch; The Life and Times of John Doe; Johnny Doe Rides Again</u>).

Place quotation marks around the titles of <u>parts</u> of whole entities such as articles from a newspaper (e.g., "Man Dies in House Fire"), chapters of a novel (e.g., "John Doe Leaves Karen"), and scenes from a motion picture (e.g., "Johnny Doe Vows to Return").

75a. *Titles Underlined (Italicized)*

Underline or italicize the titles of albums, ballets, books, compact disks, magazines, motion pictures, musicals, newspapers, novels, operas, pamphlets, periodicals, plays, poems (long), published speeches, radio series, symphonies, television series, yearbooks.

75b. When The is the First Part of a Newspaper or Periodical Title Used in Text

Ordinarily, when *a, an,* or *the* is the first word of a title, it is capitalized and underlined or italicized (e.g., A, *A*; An, *An*, The, *The*). However, there are two exceptions regarding *the*. Unless it begins a sentence, even if it is the first word in a publication's official name (e.g., The Doetown Post-Dispatch; The Doe Monthly), *the* is not capitalized or underlined (italicized) when a newspaper or periodical title is used in text (e.g., statistics reported by the Doetown Post-Disptach; quotes appearing in the Doe Monthly.)

75c. When a Geographic Name Begins a Newspaper or Periodical Title

When the name of a city, state, or locality is the first word in the official title of a newspaper or periodical, it is underlined or italicized (e.g., Virginia Daily Auto News; *Ohio Real Estate Monthly*). Otherwise, it is not (e.g., Virginia Daily Auto News; Ohio *Real Estate Monthly*).

75d. Names Underlined (Italicized)

Underline (italicize) the name of a particular aircraft (Enola Gay) or spacecraft (Atlantis), painting, sculpture, software program, train, ship. Do not underline (italicize) S.S. or U.S.S. when it precedes a ship's name (e.g., U.S.S. Jelly Bean Ride; U.S.S. *Jelly Bean Ride*). Do not underline or italicize marks of punctuation unless they are part of the actual name or title (e.g., Did you ever sail aboard the U.S.S. Jelly Bean Ride?).

75e. *Nicknames*

Given names and nicknames that have become commonly used as substitutes for given names are written the same way, with no additional punctuation.

A nickname may be introduced in one of two ways. It can be placed within quotation marks or enclosed in parentheses immediately following the given name it replaces (e.g., John "Rocky" Doe or John (Rocky) Doe. In either case, after the nickname is introduced, it is written without quotation marks or parentheses (e.g., Rocky Doe).

75f. *Word, Phrase, Number, or Letter Discussed as Itself*

Underline (italicize) a word discussed as a word (example 1), a phrase as a phrase (example 2), a number as a number (example 3), or a letter discussed as a letter (example 4, 5). Do not underline (italicize) s or 's endings (example 4, 5) or punctuation (example 2).

Examples

1. Belch is not a pleasing sounding word. (*Belch* is not a pleasing sounding word.)
2. Are you with me? is an irritating phrase. (*Are you with me?* is an irritating phrase.)
3. He wanted a 7 but he got an 11. (He wanted a *7* but he got an *11*.)
4. John should mind his Ps and Qs. (John should mind his *P*'s and *Q*'s.)
5. John should mind his ps and qs. (John should mind his *p*'s and *q*'s.)

75g. Word(s) Being Defined

Underline (italicize) a word or words being defined.

Example

John defines nebbish (*nebbish*) as one who is a feckless, effete twerp.

75h. Foreign Words and Expressions

Underline (italicize) foreign words and expressions that have not become part of the English language. A dictionary will indicate which words and expressions should be treated as foreign.

Example

Bob liked to use a ruse de querre (*ruse de querre*) whenever they played checkers.

75i. Underlining (Italics) for Emphasis

Underlining (italics) may be used to provide emphasis, but it should be employed rarely and sparingly.

Example

1. Now tell us how you really (*really*) feel, Bob.

75j. Your Own Title

Do not underline (italicize) your own title or place it in quotation marks.

75k. Titles within Quotation Marks

Place quotation marks around the titles of articles, chapters, divisions, episodes of radio and television, essays, lectures, poems (short), reports, scenes, reactions, sermons, short stories, songs.

75l. Quotation Marks with Words Used in a Unique, Ironic, or Special Way.

Quotation marks may be used to set off words whose traditional meaning has been replaced by one that is unique, ironic (see example), or special in some way.

Example

After winning $50 million in the lottery, John made a "generous" donation to his church- -$50.

75m. Do Not Use Quotation Marks with Cliches or Common Slang

Cliches should be avoided. But if one must be used, do not use quotation marks in an effort to enliven it. For example, write strong as an ox, not "strong as an ox"; quick as greased lightning, not "quick as greased lightning," etc.

Do not place quotation marks around slang terms that have come into common use. For example, it is couch potato, not "couch potato"; doggy bag, not "doggy bag," etc.

75n. What Not to Underline (Italicize) or Place within Quotation Marks

Do not underline (italicize) or place quotation marks around the titles of sacred writings or their divisions (e.g., Bible, Exodus, Old Testament, Koran, Talmud), laws (e.g., Civil Rights Act of 1964), court cases (e.g., Roe v. Wade), well-known documents (e.g., Articles of Confederation, Bill of Rights, Constitution, Declaration of Independence, Mayflower Compact, Second Amendment).

76. Who, Whom, *and* Whose

The correct use of the pronouns *who* (whoever), *whom* (whomever), and *whose* is dictated by their function in a sentence or dependent clause. When the who/whom pronoun is used in a dependent clause, its case is determined solely by its function within that clause- -not by the rest of the sentence.

Use the subjective (nominative) case *who* when the pronoun is the subject or predicate pronoun in a sentence or dependent clause.

Use the objective case *whom* when the pronoun is the object of a preposition, direct object, indirect object, and with infinitives.

Use the possessive case *whose* when the pronoun shows possession. Do not confuse *whose* (whose book is it?) with the contraction *who's* (who is).

76a. Parenthetic Expressions and the Choice of Who or Whom

Parenthetic expressions are word groups like *he believes, I am sure, did he say, we hope*, etc., that come between the who/whom pronoun and the predicate for a sentence or dependent clause.

These expressions are irrelevant when determining the correct form of the pronoun. However, they can obscure its grammatical function (subject or object) within a sentence or clause and make the choice between *who* and *whom* more difficult.

Parenthetic expressions have two defining characteristics:

1. A parenthetic expression can be deleted with little or no effect on the meaning of the full sentence or dependent clause from which it is taken.
2. A parenthetic expression has is own subject and predicate that are separate and distinct from the subject and predicate of the full sentence or dependent clause.

The same subject and predicate may be parenthetic in one instance but not in another. In each case, it is the grammatical structure that will determine whether a subject and predicate form a parenthetic expression or whether they are fundamental parts of a sentence or dependent clause. This determination is the key to selecting the correct form whenever the who/whom pronoun is used.

Quick Test

To determine whether a subject and predicate are a parenthetic expression:

Delete the words being tested.

    A. If the remaining sentence (example 1) or dependent clause (example 3) still has its own predicate, the test expression is parenthetic. Therefore, the pronoun will be the

subjective case *who*, reflecting its function as the subject of the full sentence or dependent clause.
B. If the remaining sentence (example 2) or dependent clause (example 4) is left without is own predicate, the test expression is not parenthetic. Therefore, the pronoun will be the objective case *whom*, reflecting its function as an object in the full sentence or dependent clause.

<u>Examples</u>

1. *Who*/whom did he believe was beyond any doubt?
   (The Quick Test shows that *did he believe* is a parenthetic expression because after deleting it, the full sentence still has a predicate- *-was*. Therefore, the pronoun choice is *who*, reflecting its function as the subject of the dependent clause.)
2. Who/*whom* did he believe beyond any doubt?
   (The Quick Test shows that in this instance *did he believe* is not parenthetic because deleting it leaves the full sentence without a predicate. Therefore, the choice is *whom*, reflecting its function as an object in the sentence in which *he* is the subject and *did believe* the predicate.)
3. The prosecutor said John is the only witness *who*/whom he believes is beyond doubt.
   (The Quick Test shows that *he believes* is parenthetic because after deleting it the dependent clause still has a predicate- *-is*. Therefore, the choice is *who*, reflecting its function as the subject of the clause.)

4. The prosecutor said John is the only witness who/*whom* he believes beyond doubt.
   (The Quick Test shows that in this instance *he believes* is not parenthetic because deleting it leaves the dependent clause without a predicate. Therefore, the choice is *whom*, reflecting its function as an object in the dependent clause in which *he* is the subject and *believes* the predicate.)

76b. Who/Whom, *Preposition, Infinitive, Dependent Clause*

When the object of a preposition or infinitive is a single word, and the choice is between *who* and *whom*, the correct pronoun will always be *whom* (e.g., to whom; to see whom, etc.).

However, when the object of a preposition or infinitive is not a single word but a dependent clause, the choice will be determined by the pronoun's function within that clause- -not by the preposition (examples 1,3) or the infinitive that precedes it (example 2).

Examples

1. The scholarship will be presented to (*who*, whom) makes the highest grades. (*Who* is the subject of *makes*. The object of the preposition *to* is the entire dependent clause: who makes the highest grades.)
2. George peered out the window to see (*who*, whom) had hit his car with a brick. (*Who* is the subject of *had hit*. The object of the infinitive *to see* is the entire dependent clause: who had hit his car with a brick.

3. The scholarship will be presented to (who, *whom*) he picks as the best student. (*He* is the subject, *picks* the verb, and *whom* the object is the dependent clause: whom he picks as the best student. The entire clause is the object of the preposition *to*.)

76c. Who/Whom *and Regular Infinitives*

An infinitive is not a verb. It is a verbal, one of three grammatical elements (gerunds and participles are the others) that are derived from a verb. An infinitive is formed by combining the preposition *to* with a verb*. Infinitives have special properties:

1. An infinitive is never the verb for a sentence or dependent clause.
2. An infinitive can have a subject (example 1), an object (example 2), or both (example 3).
3. Both subjects and objects of infinitives must be in the objective case (examples 1-4). *Whom* is the objective case form of the relative/interrogative pronoun who. Personal pronouns in the objective case are *me, us, you**, him, her, it,* and *them*. Nouns (example 4) have the same form for both the subjective and the objective cases.

Examples

1. My boss wants (who, *whom*) to resign?
   (As the subject of the infinitive *to resign*, the pronoun must be the objective case *whom*.)
2. My boss wants to fire (who, *whom*)?
   (As the object of the infinitive *to fire*, the pronoun must be the objective case *whom*.

3. My boss wants him to hire (who, *whom*)?
   (Because *him* is the subject and *whom* the object of the infinitive *to hire*, both pronouns must be in the objective case.
4. My boss wants the foreman to hire (who, *whom*)?
   (The noun *foreman* is the subject and the pronoun *whom* the object of the infinitive *to hire* so both must be in the objective case.)

* Recall that the preposition *to* plus a *noun* or *pronoun* (and any adjoining adjectives) forms a prepositional phrase.

** The form and spelling of the second person pronoun *you* is the same whether it is singular or plural or whether its sentence function places it in the subjective or objective case. *You* always takes a plural verb.

76d. Who/Whom *and the Infinitive* To Be

Combining the *be* form of the verb *to be** (which never takes an object) with *to* results in a unique grammatical element- -the infinitive *to be*. As with regular infinitives, the infinitive *to be* can have a subject, an object, or both.

The subject of a regular infinitive and the subject of the infinitive *to be* must always be in the objective case.

The object of a regular infinitive must always be in the objective case.

However, the object of the infinitive *to be* may be in either case- -objective or subjective- -depending on grammatical structure. The pronouns *who* and *whom* are used in the examples and are representative of how all pronouns are affected by these principles.

If the infinitive *to be* has both an object and a subject, the object must be in the objective case (example 1). However, if the infinitive *to be* has an object but is without a subject, the object must be in the subjective case (example 2).

Examples

1. In this scene, the director wants me to be (who, *whom*)?
   The pronouns, *me* as the subject and *whom* as the object of the infinitive *to be*, must both be in the objective case.)
2. In this scene, the star wants to be (*who*, whom)? (The infinitive *to be* has no subject, so its pronoun object must be in the subjective case--*who*.)

* *to be* is interchangeable with *be* as the collective term for the same irregular linking verb and its many forms (am, are, be, been, being, is, was, were).

978-0-595-36298-1
0-595-36298-2

Printed in the United States
54753LVS00001B/49-72